The University of Alabama Press
Tuscaloosa, AL 35487-0380

Theater History Studies is an official journal of the Mid-America Theatre Conference, Inc. (MATC). The conference encompasses the states of Illinois, Indiana, Iowa, Kansas, Michigan, Minnesota, Missouri, Nebraska, North Dakota, South Dakota, and Wisconsin. Its purposes are to unite people and organizations within this region and elsewhere who have an interest in theatre and to promote the growth and development of all forms of theatre.

Theatre History Studies is devoted to research in all areas of theatre history. Manuscripts should be prepared in conformity with the guidelines established in the *Chicago Manual of Style,* submitted in duplicate, and sent to Rhona Justice-Malloy, Editor, Dept. of Theatre Arts, Isom Hall 110, University of Mississippi, Box 1848, University, MS 38677-1848 or by e-mail to rjmalloy@olemiss.edu. Consulting editors review the manuscripts, a process that takes approximately four months. The journal does not normally accept studies of dramatic literature unless there is a focus on actual production and performance. Authors whose manuscripts are accepted must provide the editor with an electronic file, using Microsoft Word. Illustrations (preferably high-quality originals or black-and-white glossies) are welcomed. Manuscripts will be returned only if accompanied by a stamped, self-addressed envelope bearing sufficient postage.

This publication is issued annually by the Mid-America Theatre Conference and The University of Alabama Press.

Subscription rates for 2008 are $15 for individuals, $30 for institutions, and an additional $8 for foreign delivery. Back issues are $29.95 each. Subscription orders and changes of address should be directed to Allie Harper, The University of Alabama Press, Box 870380, Tuscaloosa, AL 35487 (205-348-1564 phone, 205-348-9201 fax).

Theatre History Studies is indexed in *Humanities Index, Humanities Abstracts, Book Review Index, MLA International Bibliography, International Bibliography of Theatre, Arts & Humanities Citation Index, IBZ International Bibliography of Periodical Literature,* and *IBR International Bibliography of Book Reviews,* the database of *International Index to the Performing Arts.* Full texts of essays appear in the databases of both *Humanities Abstracts Full Text* and *SIRS.* The journal has published its own index, *The Twenty Year Index, 1981–2000.* It is available for $10 for individuals and $15 for libraries from Rhona Justice-Malloy, Editor, Dept. of Theatre Arts, Isom Hall 110, University of Mississippi, Box 1848, University, MS 38677-1848.

THEATRE HISTORY STUDIES

VOLUME II — CONTENTS — 1982

MID-AMERICA THEATRE CONFERENCE

The Mid-America Theatre Conference is a regional affiliate of the American Theatre Association and encompasses the states of Iowa, Kansas, Minnesota, Missouri, Nebraska, North Dakota, and South Dakota. Its purposes are to unite persons and organizations within the region with an interest in theatre and to promote the growth and development of all forms of theatre.

COUNCIL AND OFFICERS

Erratum

In Volume I of *THS* the paragraph at the top of page 37 should be the final paragraph on page 38.

Let's Hear It from the Losers; or, Chekhov, Komissarzhevskaya, and *The Sea Gull* at St. Petersburg in 1896

The winners write the history of the war.
—Jefferson Davis

Eugene K. Bristow

Among the memorable events in the modern Russian theatre, few perhaps equal in significance the Moscow Art Theatre production of Anton Chekhov's *The Sea Gull* (Chaika) on the 17th of December 1898. Two months into its first season, the new theatre and its two founders had reached the turning point. They must score with this production or slip into the footnotes of history. Although their *Sea Gull* seemed bound for disaster, the triumphant response by both audience and critics ensured the establishment of the new theatre and led to new playscripts by the author. The symbol of the "sea gull," stitched to the curtain and stamped on the posters, tickets, and play programs of the Moscow Art Theatre, not only seals in visible form the inseparable linking of theatre, author, and play, but also dramatically reveals the domination of one art moment, as well as the beginning of the next, in the Russian theatre. The production of *The Sea Gull* by the Moscow Art Theatre underlined the domain of the naturalistic, subsequently refined to the realistic, movement in the proscenium arch theatre of illusion and — at the same time — predicted the introduction of the modern theatre of multiple forms, techniques, and styles.

Important events in our theatrical past are usually iced and re-iced — much as some do with day-old cake — by numerous stories associated with the events because, it seems, we like to bring back something of their original flavor and essence. Part of our task as historians of those magnificent productions of plays, however, is sorting out the numerous stories attached to each production and distinguishing the bad from the beautiful, discriminating between the false and the true, and assigning some stories to legend, others to myth, some to miscellanea, and others eventually, so the historian may hope, to the closet and dust.

Among several apocryphal stories related to the production of Chekhov's *The Sea Gull* by MKhAT in 1898 is one that has been told, and retold countless times, until it now glitters as brightly as fool's gold did, when you — as a child — first found it. In his book, Maurice Valency tells it like this.[1]

Eugene K. Bristow is Professor of Theatre and Drama in the Department of Theatre and Drama and the Russian and East European Institute at Indiana University in Bloomington. He is writing a history of the modern Russian Theatre.

Having passed the censor "with little difficulty" (p. 141), *The Sea Gull* was accepted for production at the Alexandrinsky Theatre in St. Petersburg and scheduled to open 17 October 1896 for the benefit night of the comedienne Levkeeva. Chekhov went to Petersburg from his estate outside Moscow and sat through rehearsals in early October. "He soon realized that he had cause for uneasiness. In spite of his frequent admonitions, the actors insisted on declaiming their parts as if they were acting a tragedy. Five days before the opening, the great Savina decided that the role of Nina did not suit her. and she resigned it to Vera Kommissarzhevskaya, at that time a novice. Chekhov began to feel real anxiety. For all his coaching, the actors gave no sign that they understood what was required of them. . . . Chekhov did his best to explain that his characters were simple people who must be played quietly and naturally as if they were human beings. The actors made nothing of this. The play bored them. It gave them no points to make, no grand entrances, no effective exits, no scenes of high climax. . . . They felt a momentary flush of excitement at the seventh rehearsal, when Kommissarzhevskaya's talent suddenly came to light, but it proved to be no more than a flash in the pan, and the company lapsed once more into its customary dejection. . . . *The Sea Gull* opened before a full house. The audience had come to see the buxom Levkeyeva [sic] play one of her customary funny parts. She had cannily chosen a double bill for her benefit night, first Chekhov's play, then a three-act comedy of traditional cut. When the curtain rose, the audience was puzzled, then it became impatient; soon it began to behave badly. A sharp laugh interrupted Nina's monologue in Treplev's play. A growing hum of conversation throughout the house drowned out the actor's [sic] voices. The audience had ceased to listen. The actors were terrified. The first act ended among boos and whistles and the stamping of feet. It was a disaster. Chekhov took refuge in Levkeyeva's dressing room. When the play was mercifully over, he slunk out of the theatre alone, with his coat collar up to hide his face; but he did not altogether escape detection. For four hours he walked the streets. Meanwhile, his sister and his friends grew anxious, and sent emissaries out to find him. At last, at two in the morning, he turned up at the Suvorin's [sic] where he was staying, and went directly to bed. 'If I live to be seven hundred,' he told Suvorin, 'I'll not give another play to the theatre. In this field I am a failure," (pp. 141-2). Chekhov left Petersburg that same afternoon (18 October 1896). "On the second night, the play was more thoughtfully received. But the press was almost unanimously vicious. Except for Suvorin and Avilova, none of the critics had a good word to say for *The Sea Gull*. After the third performance, which came off even better, Potapenko wired his congratulations, and wrote an enthusiastic review. It was too late. The damage was done. *The Sea Gull* labored through five performances, then it closed. When Tolstoy read it, after its publication in the December issue of *Russian Thought*, he added his venerable voice to the chorus of critical opinion: 'It is absolutely worthless. It reads like a play by Ibsen' " (pp. 142-3). Five months after the disaster in Petersburg, Chekhov could no longer escape from the knowledge that he had tuberculosis. He began spending the winters in the south, settling at last in Yalta. Another year passed. "In May 1898, when the weather turned warm, Chekhov returned once again to Moscow. . . . Immediately after his return, the wound left by that wretched evening in Petersburg was opened once again. His old friend Vladimir Nemirovich-Danchenko had written to tell him of the new theatre he had organized, and to ask his permission to include *Ivanov* and *The Sea Gull* in its repertory. . . . Chekhov replied that he had neither the desire nor the strength to experience again the anguish of the theatre" (pp. 160-1, 165). Nemirovich insisted, Chekhov resisted, but was eventually persuaded by Nemirovich to give his permission to stage his plays. And it was their production that convinced the Russian public — and even Chekhov himself — that Chekhov was indeed a playwright of great merit. In the period before the doors were opened to their production of *The Sea Gull*, the rehearsals "were going badly. There were last-minute cast changes. The actors were nervous. Chekhov's health had to be considered, in the event of another disaster, and his sister Masha pleaded hysterically with Stanislavsky to withdraw the play. It had been rehearsed twenty-six times. It was impossible to withdraw it. The day before the opening, Stanislavsky insisted on the need for more rehearsals. Nemirovich refused, whereupon Stanislavsky asked that his name be removed from the playbills as regisseur. He did not as yet understand the play, and he had absolutely no faith in it. Nevertheless, *The Sea Gull* opened on schedule on December 17. The house was far from full. The actors were frightened and, Stanislavsky later reported, the whole production smelled of Valerian drops, the usual sedative of the period. The curtain rose. . . . No one could guess how the audience was taking it. . . . Olga Knipper was ill. She had played Arkadina in a high fever. The moment the curtain came down, she fainted. The other actors began to walk off the stage dejectedly, certain that the play had failed, and the theatre was doomed. Suddenly the house exploded in a frenzy of applause" (pp. 173-4).

In short, the persuasiveness of Nemirovich, as well as the highly successful production of *The Sea Gull* at the new Moscow Art Theatre in 1898 — these were the ingredients that rescued Chekhov from oblivion as a playwright and subsequently gave him to posterity. Valency's story of *The Sea Gull*, spun out over thirty-five pages of print, is beautifully put together. It is built, as are several versions in Russian that he draws upon, very much like a thrilling melodrama. Our hero, Anton Chekhov, and his little hand of friends and loyal sister are depicted with care and sympathy. There are the villains, too, clearly evidenced in the personages of (first) Evtikhy Karpov, the mediocre regisseur at the Alexandrinsky; (second) the great actress Maria Gavrilovna Savina (1854-1915), who, foreseeing the impending disaster, trips off the stage, tossing the role of Nina Zarechnaya to the thirty-two-year-old novice, Komissarzhevskaya; (third) the buxom Elizabeta Ivanovna Levkeeva who, according to Valency, "cannily" arranges *The Sea Gull* to play before her chosen farce on the very same evening; (fourth) the other performers in the première production, who do not even try to do what Chekhov carefully tells them to do; (fifth) the doltish audience on opening night who shout down the production; (sixth) the "vicious" newspaper critics, just waiting for

Chekhov to fumble. The opening performance is a disaster, and our hero, his little band, and loyal sister trudge off to Moscow. Chekhov gives up playwriting, and perhaps "to escape the memory of his humiliation," so Valency explains, the chastened, sometime dramatist plunges "into a period of feverish activity" that culminates with "a severe hemmorrhage of the lungs" (p. 159). A happy ending to this memodrama, however, becomes possible with the arrival of that good scout, Nemirovich, who, together with the fiery leader Stanislavsky and their competent troopers at the Moscow Art Theatre, come charging out — much like Custer and the 7th Cavalry in those countless films — to rescue our hero, his little band of followers, and an hysterical sister.

As with many apocryphal stories, Valency's version contains grains of truth that glue the numerous fallacies together. Where, precisely, does our storyteller go wrong? Where does he go right? And is it possible to separate fact from fiction in his "factional" account?

Valency's first problem, and perhaps his greatest, is reading chiefly what the "winners" in Moscow have to say about the "losers" in Petersburg. His sources are limited to Nemirovich and Stanislavsky, who, together with their followers like Nikolay Efros (1867-1923), enhance the prestige of MKhAT and their own stature, as well, by beefing up negative opinion as it pertains to the Petersburg production. A second problem — by no means limited to Valency — confuses the distinction between the aims of the historian and those of the storyteller. *The Sea Gull* is, after all, only a play. It is not a matter of life and death. Until Stanislavsky — who cannot resist telling a good story — makes it so. Thus, the "failure" in Petersburg must not be repeated in Mowcow, Stanislavsky confesses in his autobiography; if it were to fail, it "could turn out fatal to the playwright himself."[2] Success in Moscow is not enough, Stanislavsky goes on; the production must result in "triumph. And if it does not, then you know that . . . your beloved playwright will die, executed by your own hands" (p. 328).

If the winners in Moscow can link the play to the very survival of its author, what on earth do the losers in Petersburg have to say for themselves? Quite a different account, as it turns out.

Anton Chekhov wrote and rewrote *The Sea Gull* over an eight month period from October 1895 to April 1896, charged Ignaty Nikolaevich Potapenko (1856-1929), a friend and fellow author, to steer the playscript through the various censorship offices, and had originally thought of giving the play to the Maly Theatre in Moscow. Having heard of Chekhov's new play, but not having read it, the famous comic actress at the Alexandrinsky in St. Petersburg, Levkeeva (1851-1904), chose it for her benefit performance (in celebration of twenty-five years on the stage), which was scheduled for Thursday 17 October 1896. Levkeeva apparently chose the play because she believed it was going to be similar to the short farces that Chekhov had written in the eighties and early nineties — farces that were extremely popular in the theatre, such as *On the Injurious Effects of Tobacco* (1886) and *The Bear* (1888). When there was obviously no role at all for Levkeeva to play in *The Sea Gull* on her own benefit night, she simply chose a three-act farce, *A Happy Day*, as the second part of a double bill. In the autumn of 1896, at the same time discussions were going on between the author and Karpov as to casting the roles, Chekhov jokingly wrote to a friend, saying that Levkeeva who was forty-five and fat was going to play his slender, 17-year-old heroine Nina Zarechnaya.[3]

Casting the play was chiefly carried on via correspondence between Chekhov and his regisseur, and the matter was settled by 4 October. Savina was cast as Nina (Chekhov's own choice); Maria Mikhaylovna Chitau (1860-?), as Masha. The casting of the female roles was apparently more difficult than casting the male roles. The first reading with the cast took place Tuesday 8 October; the opening performance had been scheduled for ten days later. Time was extremely short, Karpov recalled years later, and he put down on paper what he believed his objective had been at that time. "My hope," he wrote, "was that gifted, experienced artists, in concert, having undertaken their work with love, would at last come out the victor over this damnably difficult situation."[4]

A brief description of the performers, their training, and experience may reveal perhaps their aptitude, as well as motivation, in working on their roles. Let's begin with the regisseur, Evtikhy Pavlovich Karpov (1857-1926). Having participated in the people's movement, Karpov was arrested and imprisoned (1879-1885). Beginning in 1887, however, he worked as an actor in Yaroslavl, and — in the course of his career — he wrote twenty plays that were produced in Moscow and in Petersburg. Usually described as "a mediocre dramatist,"[5] Karpov is sometimes held to be "one of the more interesting minor playwrights of Chekhov's time, highly aware of new theatrical forms and open to original and innovative ideas."[6] In 1889 Karpov began his work as regisseur, staging plays in the provinces. He was chief regisseur at the Alexandrinsky from 1896 to 1900, returning there as regisseur in 1916 until his death.[7]

The most experienced performers at the Alexandrinsky were Davydov, Varlamov, Sazonov, and Pisarev. Born in Novomirgorod, Vladimir Nikolaevich Davydov (1849-1925) — upon completion of this education — went to Moscow, fell in love with the theatre, and began training with I. V. Samarin (1817-85) at the Maly Theatre. Playing roles in the provinces (1867-80), Davydov made his debut at the Alexandrinsky in 1880, remaining there until a year before his death. Held in high regard by the great playwright Alexander Ostrovsky, Davydov acted in a number of Chekhov's plays, including the title role in *Ivanov* (1887), Firs in *The Cherry Orchard* (1905), and Chebutykin in *The Three Sisters* (1910). Davydov originated the role of Sorin in 1896 (*TE*, II, 265-9). Son of the composer A. E. Varlamov (1801-48), Konstantin Alexandrovich Varlamov (1848-1915) performed (in his youth) in amateur theatricals, received training from A. A. Shubert, a student of the famous Mikhail Shchepkin (1788-1863), and then toured in the provinces for eight years. In 1875 he made his debut at the Alexandrinsky and remained there until his death. Varlamov played roles in different kinds of plays and in operettas and was considered exceptional in comic roles, often referred to as the "tsar of Russian laughter" (*TE*, I, 830). In the course of his career, for example, he played four different roles in *The Inspector General* (Revizor), including that of the Mayor, as well as twenty-nine roles in plays by Ostrovsky. Varlamov originated the role of Shamraev in the 1896 production of *The Sea Gull*.

Having completed his studies at the Petersburg training center (1863), Nikolay Fyodorovich Sazonov (1843-1902) joined the company at the Alexandrinsky, performing there until his death. Possessing a pleasing physical appearance, a beautiful voice, plasticity, and music talent, Sazonov had found success in the *vaudeville*, as well as in operettas, during the early phases of his career. In the seventies, however, Sazonov turned to some twenty-five roles in plays by Ostrovsky, such as the role of Murzavetsky in *Wolves and Sheep* (1875). Among his techniques was careful attention to details in characterization and business. Sazonov originated the role of Trigorin, the famous author, in *The Sea Gull* (*TE*, IV, 808). Not only an actor, but also teacher and critic, Modest Ivanovich Pisarev (1844-1905) completed a degree in law at Moscow University in 1865. He worked in the provinces as an actor, as well as in the Pushkin Theatre of A. A. Brenko (1880-82), the Theatre of Korsh (1883-84), and from 1885 in the Alexandrinsky. Among his well-known roles were Neschastlevtsev in *The Forest* and Bolshov in *It's a Family Affair — We'll Settle It Ourselves* by Ostrovsky, and Anany Yakovlev in *Bitter Fate* by Alexey Pisemsky. Pisarev originated the role of Dr. Dorn (*TE*, IV, 363-5). The youngest member of the cast, Roman Borisovich Apollonsky (1865-1928) originated the role of the young author, Treplyov, in *The Sea Gull*. In 1881 Apollonsky completed his training in the ballet division of the Petersburg theatrical training center and, in that same year, he was taken into the acting troupe at the Alexandrinsky, remaining there until his death. Having been blessed with a physical appearance often described as "brilliant" (*TE*, I, 248), a beautiful voice, and refined manners, Apollonsky usually performed roles that fell into the category of "first lover," ranging from Hamlet to Chatsky in *Woe from wit* (Gore ot uma). His best work, it seems, took place in the so-called "character" roles, such as that of Professor Storitsyn in the play of the same name by Leonid Andreev. Stanislavsky, for example, apparently gave out "rhapsodic" testimonials over Apollonsky in that role.

As to the roles of Arkadina, the actress and mother, and Polina, the wife of Shamraev, these were assigned to Dyuzhikova and Abarinova, respectively. Antonina Mikhaylovna Dyuzhikova (1853-1918) completed her education at the Petersburg training center in 1873 and made her debut at the Alexandrinsky, playing the role of Maria Andreevna in Ostrovsky's *The Poor Bride*. Other important roles were Ophelia in *Hamlet;* Beatrice in *Much Ado About Nothing;* and Katerina in Ostrovsky's *The Storm*. She retired in 1902 because of illness (*TE*, II, 601). Antonia Ivanovna Abarinova (1842-1901) studied singing in Petersburg and then in Milan and took lessons with Viardo in Paris in 1874. Originally a contralto, subsequently a mezzo-soprano, Abarinova gave concerts in cities such as Moscow, Odessa, Genoa in the period from 1861 to 1872 and performed in opera houses in Odessa and Tiflis at the end of the sixties. In 1872 she made her debut in Petersburg in a comic opera by Offenbach and was eventually taken into the imperial theatre system. From 1878 until her death, Abarinova played roles in legitimate drama. Among her best work were Natalya in *Woe from wit;* Gurmyzhskaya in *The Forest* and Ogydalova in *The Girl without a Dowry* by Ostrovsky (*TE*, I, 15).

As the regisseur Evtikhy Karpov was getting ready for the rehearsals, Chekhov was on his way to St. Petersburg. The author invited an acquaintance, Vladimir Nikolaevich Ladyzhensky (1859-1932), to go along with him, and Ladyzhensky, a poet as well as journalist, subsequently recalled that invitation. " 'Let's go take a look,' " Chekhov said, " 'at how my play is going to flop. It's not for nothing that they're staging it on the [anniversary] of the day of the train wreck.' "[8] Nine years earlier — on 17 October 1887 — the tsar's train had been wrecked. When Ladyzhinsky protested such a morose thought, Chekhov said. " 'On the contrary, it's bound to fail, it's bound to. The point is that the majority of the actors are playing it in a stereotyped style (po sablonu). The one trying to portray the author [Trigorin], then perhaps, he will be made up to look like someone of the famous literary persons and will mimic him. A great, inspired talent — it's rare, and as for communicating the mood (nastroenie) of my play, they just won't take the trouble' " (*vvs*, p. 302).

During the early rehearsal period, the regisseur Karpov was having his own troubles. Savina did not show up for the first rehearsal, but she sent a note to Karpov, saying that she was unable to play the role of Nina, but she was prepared to play the role of Masha. Karpov then asked Chitau to give up Masha. Savina showed up for the second rehearsal and walked through the role of Masha with notebook in hand, and then Savina gave up Masha, too. That left Karpov with two rehearsals gone and two roles to fill. Eventually, he persuaded Chitau to take back the role of Masha and was delighted to find that Vera Fyodorovna Komissarzhevskaya (who was Karpov's first choice to play Nina) was anxious to play the role of the "sea gull." By the time all was in order, it was the twelfth of October — five days remaining before the opening, and Chekhov himself finally dropped by to see what was going on in rehearsal. The auditorium was dark; he stayed about thirty minutes and then started to leave. The actors did not know he was in the theatre. Karpov talked to him just before he left and reported the following exchange. It was after the rehearsal of the first act.

> *KARPOV. What do you say, Anton Pavlovich?*
>
> *CHEKHOV. Not much . . . Only they're acting a lot . . . The acting could be toned down . . . Davydov [playing Sorin, the old uncle of Treplyov] and Varlamov [playing Shamraev] — they're good . . .*
>
> *KARPOV. And Vera Fyodorovna, how's she?*
>
> *CHEKHOV. In terms of her appearance, Komissarzhevskaya resembles Nina a great deal . . . but only . . . I suppose you could point out to her that the monologue must be read simpler . . . She reads it as a good actress should, but you know Nina Zarechnaya*

> *— she's a young lady in the country . . . The first time she reads it from the stage, she has cold feet, she's trembling . . . But Komissarzhevskaya is gifted. It's nothing . . . She will play it, I think . . . (Karpov, p. 66)*

At this stage in the rehearsal process, Karpov describes Chekhov in these word: "Anton Pavlovich, like a great author, is impatient, he nervously regarded the preparatory work of the actors at rehearsals, and he was very excited" (p. 66). Later on during the rehearsal, Chekhov whispered his opinions to Karpov:

> *They're not doing it properly . . . Just see how Apollonsky is walking . . . That isn't Treplyov's gait . . . He has a nervous gait . . . And Sazonov doesn't resemble a writer at all . . . What sort of a Trigorin is he, really . . . That's the "first actor," and not a writer . . . And Chitau . . . She's overacting again. My Masha is always simple . . . She is simplicity itself . . . (Karpov, p. 66)*

As Chekhov walked out of the theatre with Potapenko, his friend reported that Chekhov was depressed by what he had witnessed at the rehearsal. " 'Nothing will come out successfully,' " Chekhov said. " 'It's boring, uninteresting, it's not essential to anyone. The actors aren't arousing anyone's curiosity, and that means — they certainly won't get the audience interested' " (*vvs*, p. 354). Potapenko, who had been at the same rehearsal, was equally distressed with half the performers who did not know their lines and still read from their notebooks. Whenever Karpov reproached the actors for their weak preparation, their reply was consistent, " 'Don't worry, I will know my role' " (*vvs*, p. 354).

Karpov reports that, at subsequent rehearsals, Chekhov talked things over with the performers, giving them characteristics of each role, going over the meaning of each scene, as he himself understood the scenes. And throughout his talks with the performers, Chekhov kept repeating: " 'Everything must be simple . . . Just as you do in life itself . . . But how do you do this on stage, — I don't know . . . It would be better if I did know . . . ' " (Karpov, p. 66). By the fifth and sixth rehearsals, little by little, Karpov reports that "the general tone of the play began to appear in outline. Chekhov regarded the acting of the artists more comfortably. With every rehearsal Komissarzhevskaya continually fascinated him [Chekhov] more and more with her acting" (Karpov, p. 68). At one point, Chekhov told the regisseur: " 'She is performing Nina in such a way — just as if she were in my own soul, listening to my intonation . . . What a subtle, sensitive actress . . . And what a fresh, alive tone she has . . . Entirely special . . . ' " (Karpov, p. 68).

During the last stages of the rehearsal process, Chekhov, upon hearing a false tone, "stopped rehearsal, interrupted in the middle of a scene and, excitedly, getting mixed up, explained to the performer the meaning of the particular sentence and always added: 'The important thing, my dear friend, it must be simple . . . without theatricality . . . Completely simple . . . ' " (Karpov, p. 68). At one of the last rehearsals, probably the seventh —

possibly the eighth — the company caught fire. Potapenko claimed that such a miracle may have stemmed from the appearance of Chekhov himself at the rehearsals; whatever happened, "only actors are acquainted with, and perhaps, only Russian actors," but it was an "incomprehensible and unyielding phenomenon . . . a miracle that saves a play that seems bound for failure" (*vvs*, pp. 354-5). Potapenko describes this very special rehearsal of *The Sea Gull*.

> *Everyone pulled together and began to act. A design appeared, even something of a general [design], something resembling mood (nastroenie). When Komissarzhevskaya entered, the scene — as it were — lit up in radiance. It was, in truth, inspired acting. In the very last scene, when Nina comes to Treplyov at night, the actress rose to such heights, which she, it seems, had never achieved. No audience was in the hall, but Chekhov was there. She played for him alone and sent him into ecstasy. At this rehearsal there was something ceremonial and festive, which undoubtedly was a miracle. The Alexandrinsky actors proved that, under certain conditions, they might reach the highest achievement. (vvs, p. 355)*

As for Chekhov at the end of this very special rehearsal, all his doubts vanished — the sweet smell of success was in the air. At the general rehearsal (what we today would call a preview performance), this miracle was not repeated.

To Potapenko the response from the audience members at this "preview" performance perhaps predicted what was about to happen the following evening with the opening of *The Sea Gull*. And it did. Valency called that opening night of 17 October a disaster. And it was. Everything was wrong. Let's begin with the wrong occasion: the celebration of twenty-five years on the stage. Levkeeva was one of the most popular comic actresses of her time. In our day she may have appeared as a combination of a thinner Marie Dressler and a fatter Phyllis Diller. Eighteen years after that terrifying night, Potapenko explains Elizaveta Levkeeva this way. Some people in life strike you as inherently funny. There's something in them that is downright hilarious: the way they move, the way they talk, the way they just look at you — you know you're going to laugh and keep right on laughing. Well, says Potapenko, that was exactly what Elizaveta Levkeeva was: "in whatever she appeared, she drew laughter with her manner, with her gait, with her voice" (*vvs*, p. 357). If admirers of Levkeeva packed the house that night, what did these persons know of Anton Chekhov? Why, Anton Chekhov has been writing dozens of funny, hilarious stories for almost fifteen years. Put Levkeeva together with Anton Chekhov, so thought those persons pressing into the Alexandrinsky that night of the seventeenth, and the evening promises to bring a wealth of ridicule, fun, and laughter. And laugh they did. Then it turned to hissing, moaning, groaning, and so on. Lika Mizinova was there and walked the corridors during the intermissions to hear what people were saying. Moreover, like Russian audiences even to this day, if they were not interested in what is going on in front of them, they simply talked with their neighbors. A friend of Chekhov's overheard a complaint that perhaps is the essence of that night. Too many in the audience suspected that they had come for fast action and slapstick farce but had been sandbagged by an allegory. The complaint? " 'Why does this Apollonsky [Treplyov] carry that dead duck around with him? Really, that's a lot of nonsense!' " (Simmons, p. 368)

If the 17th of October was a disaster, what of the other four performances at the Alexandrinsky? Every single one of the remaining performances was successful. Moreover, Vera Komissarzhevskaya, who had faltered and lost her nerve on opening night, was brilliant. Every written testimony that has come down from 1896 to our day is unanimous in agreeing that the remaining four performances were successful in communicating with the audience each night. For example, the second performance of *The Sea Gull* took place five days later, on Monday 21 October. The house was not full, and a different kind of audience had come to the Alexandrinsky to see Chekhov's new play — many of them having remembered his *Ivanov* at the Alexandrinsky seven years before. Komissarzhevskaya wrote the following note to Chekhov, who was still in the dumps on his estate near Moscow.

> *I've just returned from the theatre. Anton Pavlovich, my dear friend, we've done it! Success is complete, unanimous, what it must be, just what it had to be. How much I want to see you just now, but what I'd like much more is for you to be present, and to have heard the unanimous cry: "Author." Your, no, our "Sea Gull," because I have joined my soul with her forever, our "Sea Gull" is alive, she suffers and and has faith with such ardent fervor that she will compel many persons to have faith.*[9]

And then Komissarzhevskaya closed her note with a paraphrase of one of Nina's lines in the last act ("And when I think about my profession, then I'm no longer afraid of life"), changing it to: "Do think about your profession and don't you be afraid of life" (VFK, pp. 58, 349). For the rest of that year of 1896 Chekhov continued to receive letters from persons who had seen one of the Alexandrinsky performances of *The Sea Gull* and who were moved emotionally enough to write him. Almost twenty years later Potapenko reports that, coming across persons who had seen one of those four performances (21, 24, 28 October, and 5 November 1896), he inevitably found those persons, in his words, "become excited just as if it were yesterday [and they say]: 'No, but *The Sea Gull* . . . You understand? With Komissarzhevskaya . . . You know it was something unparalleled . . . ' " (*vvs*, p. 349).

Even though Karpov vigorously protested its removal from the repertory of the Alexandrinsky, *The Sea Gull* closed in early November 1896. In that same month, however, a highly-successful production of the play took place in Kiev and, before the year was over, there occurred another successful production in Taganrod, Chekhov's home city. Successful productions of *The Sea Gull* continued in provincial cities throughout Russia in 1897 and 1898.[10]

In 1898, too, it received the first of many successful productions outside Russia — in Prague (*Let*, p. 537). In 1897 Suvorin published Chekhov's collected plays which included his *Uncle Vanya*, and it too received productions in the provinces: Odessa, Tiflis, Kiev, and so on. "By the end of 1898," as Karlinsky reports, "royalties from these two plays represented a sizable portion of Chekhov's income" (p. 324).

In December of 1898 came the highly-successful production of *The Sea Gull* at the Moscow Art Theatre and, in the following year, an equally successful production of *Uncle Vanya*. These productions, together with the fact that Chekhov fell in love with — and eventually married — the leading actress at MKhAT, Olga Knipper, were the chief reasons that Chekhov wrote two additional plays (*The Three Sisters* in 1901 and *The Cherry Orchard* in 1904) for MKhAT before his untimely death in July of 1904.

What of Komissarzhevskaya? She quickly became Russia's most popular actress, and on her tours at the turn of the 20th century, her own production of *The Sea Gull* was performed in provincial cities. Moreover, in her own theatre in 1905, she produced *The Sea Gull* in St. Petersburg, and to her theatre she brought Vsevolod Meyerhold in 1906 who staged several productions of symbolist plays in that year and in 1907. It may well be an historical irony that Meyerhold (who played Treplyov at MKhAT in 1898) introduced in Russia the "new forms" that Treplyov calls for in *The Sea Gull*. One of the last messages that Komissarzhevskaya sent to Moscow shortly before her death in 1910 was a telegram to the Moscow Student Society in the name of Anton Chekhov. It consisted of a line of dialogue from Nina's monologue in *The Sea Gull*, Act I: "In the whole universe only the spirit, and the spirit alone, endures — constant and immutable." And Komissarzhevskaya signed it "The Sea Gull" (VFK, pp. 178, 398).

NOTES

[1]*The Breaking String; The Plays of Anton Chekhov* (New York: Oxford Univ. Press, 1966). All further references to this work appear in the text.

[2]K. S. Stanislavskij, *Moja žizn' v iskusstve* [My life in art], 3d ed. (Moscow: Academia, 1936), p. 328. All further references to this work appear in the text.

[3]A. P. Čexov, *Polnoe sobranie sočinenij i pisem v tridcati tomax* (Moscow: Izd-vo "Nauka", 1976), VI, 181.

[4]Evt. P. Karpov, ed., *Sbornik pamjati V. F. Kommissarževskoj* [A collection of memoirs about V. F. Komisssarzhevskaya] (Spb., 1911), p. 61. All further references to this work appear in the text.

[5]Ernest J. Simmons, *Chekhov: A Biography* (Boston: Little, Brown, 1962), p. 366. All further references to this work appear in the text.

[6]Simon Karlinski, *Anton Chekhov's Life and Thought* (Berkeley: Univ. of California Press, 1973), pp. 282-3. All further references to this work appear in the text.

[7]*Teatral'naja Enciklopedija* [Theatrical encyclopedia] (Moscow, 1965), IV, 1158-9. All further references to this work appear in the text, under the initials, *TE*.

[8]*A. P. Čexov v vospominanijax sovremennikov* [A. P. Chekhov in the recollections of (his) contemporaries] (Moscow, 1960), p. 302. All further references to this work appear in the text, under the intitials, *vvs*.

[9]Vera Fedorovna Komissarževskaja, *Pis'ma aktrisy* [Letters of the actress] (Leningrad-Moscow, 1964), p. 58. All further references to this work appear in the text, under the initials, *VFK*.

[10]N. I. Gitovič, *Letopis' žizni i tvorcestva A. P. Čexova* [A chronicle of the life and creative work of A. P. Chekhov] (Moscow, 1955), pp. 429-538, *passim*. All further references to this work appear in the text, under the initials, *Let*.

SOURCES CONSULTED

Text of the play

The standard Russian texts of Chekhov's plays are found in A. P. Chekhov, *Polloe sobranie sočinenij i pisem v dvadcati tomas* [The complete collected works and letters in twenty volumes], Moscow: GOSLITIZDAT [State publishing house for belles lettres], 1944-51. In 1974, a new edition of Chekhov's complete works and letters in thirty volumes was initiated and is scheduled for completion in 1982; volumes 12 and 13, bound together, contain his plays written in the period from 1889 to 1904 and were published in 1978. In addition to these standard sources, the following editions of Chekhov's works and letters were consulted.

Anton Chekhov's Plays. Trans. and ed. Eugene K. Bristow. New York: Norton, 1977. (A Norton Critical Edition)

Čajka (*The Seagull*). Ed. w/an Introduction and Notes by P. Henry. Chicago: Russian Language Specialities, 1965. (Bradda edition in Russian)

Sobranie sočinenij v dvenadcati tomax [Collected works in twelve volumes]. Moscow: GOSLITIZDAT, 1963.

Letters and memoirs in Russian

Gitovič, N. I. *Letopis' žizni i tvorcestva A. P. Čexova* [A chronicle *of the life and creative work of A. P. Chekhov*]. Moscow: GIKHL, 1955 (herein cited as *Let*).

Iz arxiva A. P. Čexova [Out of A. P. Chekhov's archives]. Moscow, 1960.

Karpov, Evt. P., ed. *Sbornik pamjati V. F. Kommissarževskoj* [A collection of memoirs about V. F. Komissarzhevskaya]. Spb., 1911.

Komissarževskaja, Vera Fedorovna. *Pis'ma aktrisy: vospominanija o nej; materialy* [Letters of the actress; recollections about her; materials]. Leningrad-Moscow: Izd-vo "Iskusstvo," 1964 (herein cited as VFK).

Koni, Anatolij Fedorivič. *Vospominanija o Čexova* [Recollections about Chekhov]. Leningrad, 1925.

Literaturnoe nasledstvo [Literary heritage], vol. 68, A. P. Čexov. Moscow-Leningrad, 1960.

Nemirovič-Dancenko, V. I. *Iz prošlogo* [Out of the past]. Moscow: GOSLITIZDAT, 1936.

______________. *Izbrannye pis'ma* [Selected letters]. Moscow: "Iskusstvo," 1979. 2 vols.

Rudnickij, K., ed. *O Komissarževskoj; zabytoe i novoe. Vospominanija; stat'i; pis'ma* [About Komissarzhevskaya; the forgotten and the new. Recollections; essays; letters]. Moscow, 1965.

Sbornik pamjati V. F. Komissarževskoj [A collection of memoirs about V. F. Komissarzhevskaya]. Moscow, 1931.

Stanislavskij, K. S. *Moja žizn' v iskusstve* [My life in art]. 3d ed. Moscow: Academia, 1936.

Stroeva, M. N. *Čexov i Xudožestvennyj teatr* [Chekhov and the art theatre]. Moscow: "Iskusstvo," 1955.

______________. *Režisserskie iskanija Stanislavskogo, 1898-1917* [Directorial strivings of Stanislavsky, 1898-1917]. Moscow: Izd-vo "Nauka," [Publishing house of "Science"], 1973.

Surkov, E. D., ed. *Čexov i teatr: pis'ma, fel'etony, sovremenniki o Čexova-dramaturge* [Chekhov and theatre: letters, newspapers (topical satire), contemporaries on Chekhov — playwright]. Moscow, 1961.

A. P. Čexov v vospominanijax sovremennikov [A. P. Chekhov in the recollections of (his) contemporaries]. Ed. N. I. Gitovič and I. V. Fedorova. Moscow: GOSLITIZDAT, 1960 (herein cited as *vvs*).

Biographical and critical studies

Hingley, Ronald. "Appendix III: *The Seagull*." In vol. II of *The Oxford Chekhov*. Trans. and ed. Ronald Hingley. London: Oxford Univ. Press, 1967, pp. 334-53.

______________. *A New Life of Anton Chekhov*. New York: Alfred A. Knopf, 1976.

Karlinsky, Simon. *Anton Chekhov's Life and Thought: Selected Letters* and Commentary. Trans.

Henry Heim and Simon Karlinsky. Selection, Introduction, and Commentary Simon Karlinsky. Berkeley: Univ. of California Press, 1973.
Kugel', Aleksandr R. *Teatral'nye portrety* [Theatrical portraits]. Petrograd, Moscow, 1923.
Llewellyn Smith, Virginia. *Anton Chekhov and the Lady withn the Dog*. London: Oxford Univ. Press, 1973.
Nosova, Valerija Vasil'evna. *Komissarževskaja* (in Russina). Moscow, 1964.
Pitcher, Harvey. *The Chekhov Play; A New Interpretation*. New York: Harper & Row, 1973.
______________________. *Chekhov's Leading Lady; A Portrait of the Actress Olga Knipper*. London: John Murray, 1979.
Rayfield, Donald. *Chekhov: The Evolution of His Art*. New York: Barnes & Noble, 1973.
Řybakova, Julija Petrovna. *Komissarževskaja* (in Russian). Leningrad, 1971.
Šax-Azizova, T. K. *Čexov i zapadno-evropejskaja drama ego vremeni* [Chekhov and western European drama of his time]. Moscow: "Nauka," 1966.
Simmons, Ernest J. *Chekhov: A Biography*. Boston: Little, Brown, 1962.
Tal'nikov, David Lazarevič. *Komissarževskaja* (in russian). Moscow-Leningrad, 1939.
Teatral'naja Enciklopedija [Theatrical encyclopedia]. Editor-in-chief P. A. Markov. Moscow, 1961-67 (herein cited as *TE*). 5 vols. plus supplement.
Valency, Maurice. *The Breaking String; The Plays of Anton Chekhov*. New York. Oxford Univ. Press, 1966.

Nikolai Evreinov

Mysteries of the Self: The Visionary Theatre of Nikolai Evreinov

SPENCER GOLUB

When the definitive chronicle of theatre in Russia's Golden Age (c. 1905-25) is written, a special place in the artistic hierarchy will have to be found for Nikolai Evreinov, among the most versatile and significant, if not to all tastes the most profound, of the theatrical innovators of this era. Soviet critics and historians have dismissed Evreinov as having been a lightminded aesthete and apolitical formalist. His emigration to Paris in 1925, where he lived with his wife until his death in 1953, did little to illuminate Western critics as to the importance of this strangely paradoxical figure. His plays seemed to have developed from Pirandellian conventions, his directorial approaches, less familiar in the West than his plays, from Gordon Craig and Vsevolod Meyerhold, his aesthetics from Oscar Wilde. The confused chronology which made Evreinov seem beholden to artists whom he in fact anticipated persisted until the point that history passed him by.

Western scholars persist in invoking the trusted model which places Stanislavsky at one end of the theatrical spectrum and Meyerhold at the other with Vakhtangov, Tairov and others in the middle to explain the broad scope of theatrical innovation in this complex period. This does not so much foster inaccuracy as it does oversimplification. In the first place, it makes the alignment of these and other theatrical artists a bit too exact and in the second, it suggests that theatrical experimentation in this period was largely a reaction to or against the work of Konstantin Stanislavsky. Finally, it tends to make us impatient in our consideration of other Russian artists who do not fit neatly into this model, and so faced either with discarding the model or cutting short discussion of the troublesome artists, we invariably opt for the latter. Such has been the case with Evreinov, who despite the fact that he was on equal footing with the aforementioned artists in their day has been eased out of the golden pantheon over the course of the last half-century.

It is not difficult to understand why Evreinov has proven to be so troublesome. A theatricalist like Meyerhold but with a Stanislavskian sense of verisimilitude in art, Evreinov prided himself on being nobody's disciple, a self-proclaimed original and "aristocrat of the theatre," an anti-Stanislavskian and an anti-Meyerholdian, an aesthete and a popularizer whose work as dramatist, theorist, director and historian ranged from the quasi-scientific to the whimsical and grotesque. Evreinov revealed little of his true personality, choosing instead to hide behind a created persona. His substantial writings were more philosophical than craft-based, addressing

Spencer Golub is Assistant Professor of Drama in the Department of Drama at the University of Virginia.

what he felt to be the major issues confronting theatre and society. He left no cohesive body of ideas regarding acting and directing, like those that have solidified the reputations of so many of his contemporaries. His highly subjective approach to art has made both his value and intentions seem suspect.

Evreinov's work embraced the twin polarities between which the history of the modern theatre unfolds and is defined — theatre as illusion (lies like truth) and theatre as event (a present-tense reality transcending the boundaries of art). Leaning more often toward the latter, Evreinov's was ultimately a visionary theatre, always the most difficult to understand and accept. This article will seek to explore the nature and scope of Evreinov's theatrical vision, some misconceptions which surround it and its implications for a theatre still very much in search of itself.

Nikolai Nikolaevich Evreinov (1879-1953) was representative of the paradoxical temper of "the epoch of beautiful romanticism" which characterized the period between the abortive and successful Russian Revolutions of 1905 and 1917.[1] St. Petersburg was alive with the spirit of masquerade, demonstrated most dramatically in the reclamation of the commedia dell'arte by artists and scholars alike. Here antic and grotesque images of mortality cavorted in often cynical tales of illicit love and betrayal, masked by a facade of romantic idealism. Here the ridiculous mingled with the sublime, essences were distilled from business both broad and mundane, confusion and even death threatened but harmony and lightmindedness prevailed. The ringmaster for this metaphysical circus of human error and travail was the trickster-chameleon Harlequin, who with one wave of his slapstick, could transform himself and his world at will, could turn men's wills toward God or the Devil.

The commedia dell'arte and Harlequin in particular had an appeal bordering upon the mystical for a society on the brink of transformation and uncertain as to where change would lead — transcendance or destruction. The harshness of its present reality and the uncertainty of its future led Russian society in search of more meaningful foundations to replace the social, moral and philosophical moorings from which it had broken free. The Symbolist poets, led by Vyacheslav Ivanov, sought via sound and rhythm to break through phenomenal reality to the noumenal reality beyond and to rediscover via congregate action and myth creation a societal dream lost to modern man since antiquity. The search for essences was a search for ultimate truth.

While such theatrical innovators as Meyerhold had themselves painted in the costumes of commedia masks, Evreinov went so far as to proclaim: "I am Harlequin, and as Harlequin I shall die."[2] Like the commedia, Evreinov too was preoccupied with mortality, his own and society's at large. He was drawn to those societies of the distant past whose primitive celebratory faith allowed them to live closer to death, whose sacred and profane rituals represented a sort of dance with death at the razor's edge. For Evreinov, the commedia masks embodied both the reality of man's transitory existence and the promise of his transcendance, his tragic condition and his antic spirit. It was, for Evreinov, the perfect symbol for a life in art and life as art.

For Evreinov, as for Harlequin, the process of transformation was everything, and so he spent more time searching for origins and evolving towards theoretical ends than in reaching actual conclusions, which he thought to be illusory in any case: "Hegel holds that when it comes to *idea*, the only important thing is the process, that the 'result' is only a lifeless corpse, forsaken by the living soul by the tendency . . ."[3]

Evreinov saw theatre not only as the living embodiment of man's transient condition and the noblest expression of his striving toward transcendence, but as the only salvation for society at large, a new religion which would reintroduce man to his instincts and society to its essences. In the process, life would be preserved and also made more livable, seasoned by the spice of theatricality. Evreinov consciously reinvented himself as the living embodiment of this idea, merging his own identity with the theatre's as the Harlequin-Christ, high priest in the service of the new god Theatrarch. Although it sometimes seemed that he was more ambitious for himself than for the theatre which he served and that the mask which he had adopted for his task had totally absorbed the face of the real man underneath, Evreinov never really forfeited his theatrical vision, nor did he lose sight of his vision's importance for society. Once one understands the theoretical underpinnings of Evreinov's approach to the theatre, it becomes clear that all of the work in his multi-faceted career was remarkably of a piece.

It was as a theatre philosopher that Evreinov wanted most to be remembered. His plays were written and productions staged primarily to demonstrate the theories which he consistently developed and tenaciously clung to during the course of his career. Evreinov's three major theories — monodrama, the theatre for oneself, and the theatre in life — form a sort of Chinese box-puzzle relationship, each succeeding theory embodying the one(s) before.

Evreinov introduced his theory of monodrama in a public lecture delivered at the Literary-Artistic Circle in Moscow, December 16, 1908, and later repeated in St. Petersburg at the Theatrical Club (February 21, 1909), and at the Dramatic Theatre of V. F. Komissarzhevskaya (March 4, 1909). It was printed in condensed form in the journal, *Theatre and Art* (March-April, 1909), and in its entirety as *An Introduction to Monodrama* (Vvedenie v. monodramu, 1909).

In what he called his "apology for theatricality," Evreinov argued that theatre was theatre, and was not meant to be used as a school, temple, podium or mirror reflecting reality, as his contemporaries had maintained. That theatre has lost its sense of identity, its theatricality, can be attributed to an unhealthy reliance on literature and convention.[4] It is not enough to do away with the footlights and Stanislavsky's mythical "fourth wall." The theatre must destroy the footlights, which continue to burn in the mind of the spectator, preventing him from entering completely into the drama onstage.

Evreinov believed that the spectator will relate only to that stage action which he can call *his* drama, which he can co-experience with the character in the play as if *he*, the spectator, were playing the role. The conventional play dissipates the spectator's concentration by asking him to divide his at-

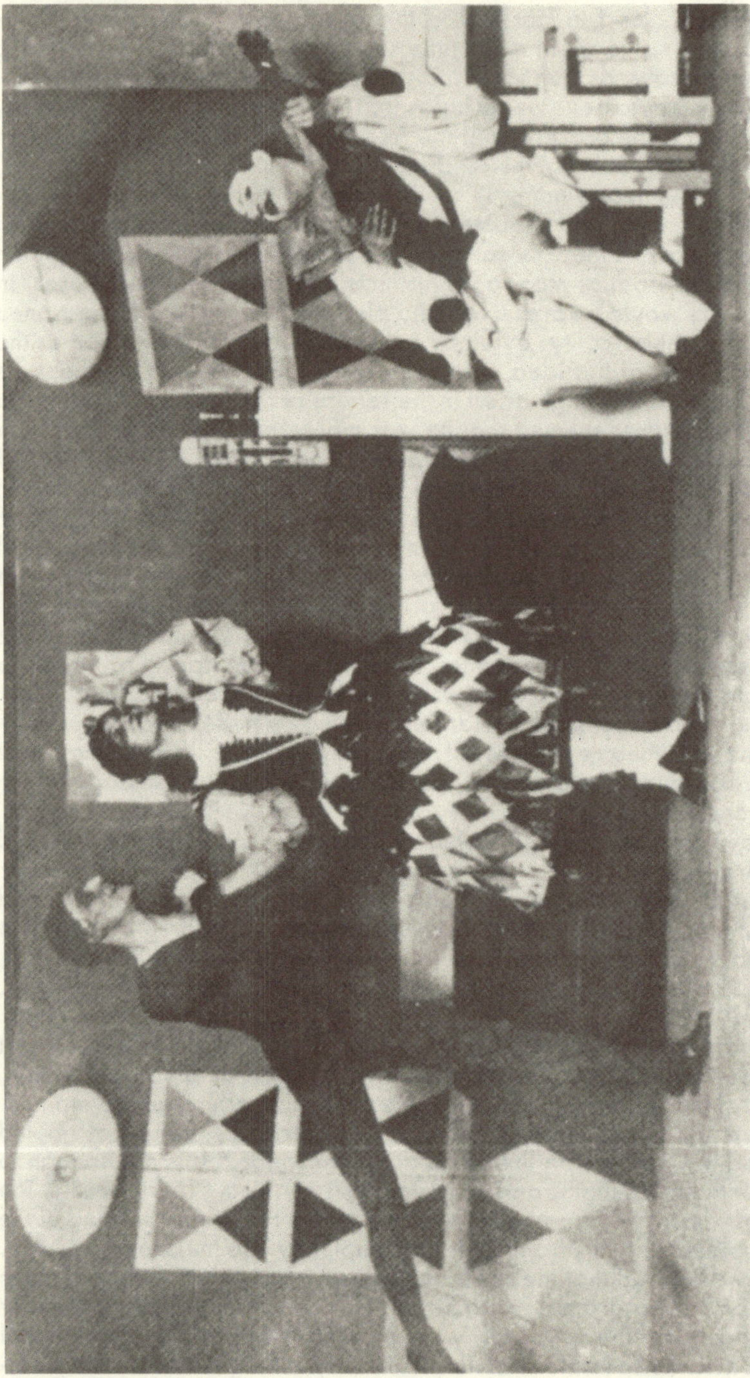

La Mort Joyeure by Evreinov as directed by Jacques Copeau at the Vieux Colombier in 1921.

tention among a number of different characters and to adopt, to a limited extent, their points of view. The result is that the spectator, whose attention has been spread too thin, becomes a passive observer.

In monodrama, we are given a single hero with whom to identify, and he is reinforced by all of the events and other characters onstage. The spectator can readily absorb the unified view being presented onstage, namely the world as filtered through the prism of the hero's consciousness. The spectator is meant to co-experience each new sensation, each new perception with the hero. The hero's drunkenness is suggested to the spectator by projecting circles of green light onstage, his dizziness by causing the scenery to sway, and so on to express his various states of mind. Stage properties are to be treated as if they were circulating in the hero's blood and so may change size, color and shape. All of this is necessary, in Evreinov's opinion, because we listen more with our eyes than with our ears. He believed, as did many of the theatrical innovators who were his contemporaries, that words constitute an insufficient mode of expression in the theatre.

Critical reaction to Evreinov's theory was immediate and vociferous, attacking its vagueness and vagaries. Most of the criticism focused on monodrama's central concept — co-experiencing. It was the opinion of some that such an arrangement between character and spectator would destroy the latter's aesthetic distance. Evreinov countered that only through monodrama could the spectator experience a moment of true "aesthetic significance," a complete impression, rather than the fragmented one which conventional drama provides.[5]

Some critics argued that co-experiencing could have ludicrous and unfortunate results. We know that if the hero goes to sleep or is depressed, the stage may be plunged into darkness. But what happens to the spectator if the hero is hit over the head with a stick? If this question seems facetious, it does nevertheless draw attention to the fact that Evreinov never made it clear just how far he wanted his concept of co-experiencing to go, and how it would be affected beyond the several instances which he cited.

It was said,too, that Evreinov's eagerness to mingle stage and audience abnegated the responsibility for creation to the spectator.[6] Evreinov answered that monodramas were to be fully scripted, carefully staged and scrupulously rehearsed performances in which the audience would play an important but limited role. It seems ironic that the perceptions of the audience, the nominal co-creator of the theatrical event, were more carefully manipulated in monodrama than in a conventional stage piece. Ultimately, increased audience involvement is not really synonymous with audience freedom or creativity.

Another criticism of monodrama as a theoretical concept was that it forces us to sacrifice our objectivity as regards the hero. Whereas in a conventional play we learn much about him from what others say, in monodrama these other characters are all shaped by the hero's imagination and perceptions.[7] Who, then is to tell us about him? Evreinov replied that in any play, we are essentially seeing the character from a single subjective point of view, the author's. He cited as examples, Pushkin's *Tales of Belkin* , Robert Browning's *The Ring and the Book*, and Griboedov's *Woe from Wit*. All of the characters in Griboedov's play, with the exception of Chatsky, who represents the author, are filtered through the creative "I" of the author/hero and made to seem as grotesque to us as they do to him.[8] So why not accept this as a condition of art in general and allow the artist free rein to explore the power of this impulse in conscious agreement with his audience?

Evreinov was further accused by some of trying to ease the audience and the actor out of the theatre, a charge to which innovative artists of the day were extremely sensitive, because it was made so frequently. But this was not Evreinov's intention. What Evreinov wanted was to break down the concept of audience as an entity, separate from the dramatic action. For him, theatre flowed into life and life into theatre, with each of us serving both as actor and audience member. But this concept was not yet fully developed in Evreinov's mind, and monodrama, which was a step in the development of his theatre in life philosophy, was treated according to its own merits or demerits.

Of Evreinov's several experiments with monodrama, by far the most unique and the most farreaching in its implications was *In the Stage-Wings of the Soul* (V kulisakh dushi), produced at St. Petersburg's Crooked Mirror Theatre on October 21, 1912. While failing to live up to Evreinov's judgment as being "the most original play in the history of the world theatre," its significance is still being pondered by scholars such as Martin Esslin who saw it as a precursor to Samuel Beckett's particular brand of absurdist theatre.[9]

The play, originally thought by the Crooked Mirror Theatre's management to be unstageable, takes place entirely inside a man's body. M. P. Bobyshev's set for the original production featured a gigantic spinal column upstage, a complex of nerves, a large heart, lungs and other vital organs which moved rhythmically throughout the play, in keeping with the mood expressed by the action and in time to the music. Evreinov records that when the curtain went up, revealing the set, a lady in the audience fainted and had to be carried out of the auditorium.[10]

The play appeared on a bill of "tragifarces," a suitable name for Evreinov's dramaturgical fare in general. One critic likened its mixture of tragedy and comedy to blending wine with poison.[11] *In the Stage-Wings of the Soul* was the perfect theatrical vehicle for Evreinov's theory. Its simple, melodramatic tale of a man who abandons his wife and child for a cafe singer, only to be left by her and driven to suicide, is infused with irony and has all the hallmarks of the monodramatic form. The cast of characters includes the hero's three Selves — the rational, emotional and eternal — as well as the subjective images of the Songstress and the Wife which they summon up.

The rational and emotional Selves are in constant conflict, co-existing in an adversary relationship, while the eternal Self remains aloof. Naturally, the rational Self demands that the man return to his wife and child, while the emotional Self urges him to forsake his boring existence and run away with the Songstress. The emotional Self depicts the Songstress as a gay and seductive young woman who sings in French and dances, while the man's heart beats joyfully in time. The rational Self counters with a grotesque caricature of the Songstress, forty years old with ingrown toenails, corns on her feet, a wig, falsies and false teeth. She gums her words and "prances about with all the grace of some old nag being sent off to the glue factory."[12]

As a pleasant alternative, the rational Self offers an image of the man's wife as an ideal mother, rocking her baby in her arms and singing a gentle lullaby. But the emotional Self calls this a "crude idealization" and presents his image of the Wife as "a sharp-tongued petty bourgeoise with a slovenly chignon and dressed in a shabby dressing gown covered with coffee stains." This less than ideal image proceeds to berate the man as a drunken atheist who loves to philosophize, but is really as stupid as a log.[13]

The "grotesque caricatures" and "crude idealizations," offered by the Selves, are equally true and untrue. In an imperfect world, everything is relative. Unable to reconcile his internal conflict, the man shoots himself through the heart, an event symbolized by red ribbons emerging through a large, gaping hole in the onstage organ. As the man dies, darkness descends and the Conductor enters with a lighted lantern. The two combatant Selves having been silenced, the eternal Self is now awakened from his sleep and instructed by the Conductor to change here for "Newville." Man is ready for the next step in his transformation, moving toward that time when he will become, according to Evreinov, an image of the Deity in his transparent mask and be happy.[14]

"Monodrama" as a form was ultimately outstripped by the cinema (especially the German expressionist cinema) which it anticipated. Aside from the continued importance of the "monodramatic" perspective in Evreinov's later work as director and dramatist and the evolution of this idea into his later theories, the form itself has implications for us today. Among its contributions to the modern theatre can be listed the following:

1) the idea of the play's protagonist being split into several selves impersonated by different actors, the concept of a divided self serving itself as a statement on the condition of modern man.

2) ultra-subjectivism — the tale told from the protagonist's point of view, literally from the inside.

3) this ultra-subjectivism reflected in the transformation of scenic elements.

4) the physicalization of the abstract mental process of a human being and the resultant de-mystification of that process: We are machines that function and malfunction depending upon the input from our systems and how well our systems manage to process it.

There is an inherent tension in *Stage-Wings* between this idea and the acute egoism which seems to inform this subjective point of view. Man is the center of the universe and yet he is as a physical being only a bit player in his own life's drama. Evreinov managed to deflate in characteristically ironic fashion the Freudian-soaked consciousness of a Stanislavsky, who saw man as a complex spiritual being. The purposely cliched romantic plot likewise parodied Stanislavsky's well-known sentimentalism. The very idea of going inside the protagonist's heart and mind made the Stanislavskian school of psychological realism seem absurd. The scent of absurdism which arose from this rather unusual theatrical stew still effectively titillates our senses today.

This seemingly overripe aesthetic statement, spoofing then current scientific developments even as it satirized man's more irrational melodramatic tendencies, embodies the sense of romanticism dying into science that one gets in all of Evreinov's work, a tragicomic paradoxical tone like that found in a harlequinade. Like Evreinov's other theories and their artistic manifestations, monodrama was concerned with the drama of being and the search for the ultimate truths of the human condition. Like Sartre after him, Evreinov located the metaphorical hell of other people within the soul, where your several selves *are* those other people, engaging in an often vituperative dialectical combat for the right to determine your choices.

All creative work for Evreinov was a function of personality. His second major theory, "the theatre for oneself," set forth in his published works, *The Theatre as Such* (Teatr, kak takovoi, 1912) and *The Theatre for Oneself, Parts 1-3* (Teatr dlya sebya, 1915-17), picked up where the theory of monodrama left off.

Evreinov posited the belief that man's thoughts and actions are governed by a prepotent, pre-aesthetic will to play, to transform himself and the world at large.[15] He was fascinated by such historical personages as Napoleon, Oscar Wilde, Aubrey Beardsley, Felicien Rops, Mikhail Nesterov and Grigory Rasputin among others and by such fictional characters as Robinson Crusoe, Don Quixote and Raskolnikov whose lives and very being represented a spirited protest against the domination of man by mundane reality, the triumph of subjective judgment and self-dramatization. These artists of the theatre for oneself ran the gamut from the spiritual (the religious painter Nesterov) to the decadent (Rops, Beardsley, Wilde), from transformers of real landscapes into spiritual planes (Nesterov) to transformers of the divine female form into a heightened sexuality transcending conventional aesthetic and moral judgment (Rops), from transformers of life into art (Wilde) to transformers of the lives of millions (Napoleon, Rasputin). Theatre for oneself justified self-expression at all costs.[16]

These practitioners of theatre for oneself, among whom Evreinov numbered himself, were what he called "aristocrats of the theatre" in that they had found within themselves the power for re-making the world in their own image. But, said Evreinov, we all have within us this potential, as can be seen in the play of children and primitive savages. We have only to get in touch with our instincts and give ourselves over to them without inhibition.[17]

Evreinov recognized that this idea could be taken to extreme and even damaging lengths. He discussed such possibilities under the headings "erotic theatre for oneself" and "excessive theatre for oneself." By "erotic," Evreinov was referring to sex play, especially the courting ritual harmlessly manifested in such festive pastimes as ballroom dancing — but taking a more dangerous turn in sado-masochistic rituals. Significantly, Evreinov made the "love comedy," Kraft-Ebbing's term for the discreet behavior of the female and the quasi-conquest by the male in courtship, the core of nearly all his dramatic works, using as his paradigm the classic romantic triangle of Harlequin, Columbine and Pierrot.

The concepts of "erotic" and "excessive" theatre for oneself were to some extent overlapping. Evreinov gave as an example the subtlest form of both — autoeroticism, narcissism born of extreme subjectivism. One can, in a sense, see this condition embodied in Evreinov's theory of monodrama, although this concept was somewhat saved by its creator's sense of irony.[18]

In discussing the excessive theatre for oneself, Evreinov admitted that the criminal nature of all theatre, beginning in lies and ending in illusion, is here magnified by the intrusion and pervasiveness of the creator's personality:

> *. . . here norms and rules no longer exist like sticks in the wheels of our fantasy! Here one can no longer ascertain what is forbidden, illicit or unlawful! This is the realm of our "transforming I," a minute ago a prisoner . . . now authoritatively turning the merest "nothing" into "everything," and this "everything" is superior to all else because it is my "everything," with my boundaries, my spirit, my Logos!*[19]

A logical extension of the theory of monodrama, the excessive theatre for oneself led Evreinov into a consideration of theatre as a metaphorical forum for crime and punishment and ultimately into a new, modern moral dimension.

In his notes for a series of lectures entitled "The Theatre and the Scaffold" (Teatr i èshafot, date unknown), Evreinov seemed to foreshadow Artaud's theatre of cruelty. Invoking images taken from the Spanish Inquisition and the French Revolution, as well as from the circus and the grand guignol, Evreinov spoke of man's need and desire to witness real or symbolic torture, its hypnotic power upon the spectator, moving him to pity and fear in the extreme, and its therapeutic value. Although his research into this concept was voluminous, stretching back to its origin in the scapegoat of Ancient Greek ritual, Evreinov did not develop the scaffold metaphor beyond these lecture notes. However, he did incorporate the idea of the curative power of theatre into his major theory of the theatre in life, the culmination of his theoretical work.[20]

The theatre in life was really only the theatre for oneself expanded to encompass entire cultures and societies. It has become a sort of generic term used to describe Evreinov's overall theoretical position. The theory of "the theatre in life" posited the Schopenhauerian idea of life as presentation of self, grounded in man's will to theatre, which was in turn an outgrowth of man's apprehension of his own dualistic nature of body and soul. On first noticing that the world of his dreams and the world of his waking reality were different, primitive man came to realize that the one must have been staged by his spiritual "I," the soul, as opposed to the other which was staged by the physical "I" of the conscious mind-body. His determination to stage such wonderful dramas as part of a conscious process resulted in the birth of theatre.[21]

A montage of foreign language editions of Evreinov's *The Chief Thing*.

Evreinov, like Oscar Wilde, took this one step further, proclaiming that the world was nothing more than inert matter until we reanimate it via art, and the truest art, that is the form closest to our natural instinct, is one in which we reanimate via ourselves. This "theatre for oneself" transforms each of us, as actor/creator, into a Nietzschean superman. We are as big as our dreams.[22] By focusing upon the realization of this ideal, man in general and Evreinov in particular accomplishes the Symbolist goal of going beyond a mere philosophy of art to discover a guiding principle for one's life. When an entire culture or society engages in theatre for oneself, the result is theatre in life, with all men and women as actor/creators, aristocrats, administering to individual and societal ills with the curative power of the theatre.[23]

Of the many plays which Evreinov wrote, his crowning achievements were those which sought to dramatize most directly the theory of the theatre in life. *The Chief Thing* (Samoe glavnoe, 1920[24]) has been produced in twenty-seven languages in twenty-five countries, most notably at Pirandello's theatre in Rome (1924), New York's Theatre Guild (1926) and Charles Dullin's Theater de l'Atelier in Paris (1926). The play depicts the coming of the Paraclete, foretold in the Bible, who preaches the doctrine "transfiguration through transformation," salvation via the will to theatre. This message was reiterated in the final two parts of Evrienov's theatre-in-life trilogy, *The Ship of the Righteous* (Korabl pravednykh, 1924) and *The Theatre of Eternal War* (Teatr vechnoy voiny, 1928).[25]

The widening scope and influence, inherent in Evreinov's definition of theatre, had great philosophical as well as practical implications. In his work as a director, Evreinov sought to transform theatre's spatial dimensions to encompass the grandeur of his conception, collapsing space in on itself in monodrama so as to see the world through the mind's eye and expanding actor-audience consciousness beyond the boundary of the curtain line in the theatre in life, an idea borne out by his productions at the Ancient Theatre and by his work with the Soviet mass spectacle.

Evreinov first came to public attention as a director through his work at the Dramatic Theatre of V. F. Komissarzhevskaya (1908) in St. Petersburg, where he replaced another visionary, Vsevolod Meyerhold, as Artistic Director. Thus began a lifelong enmity between the two men, producing in Evreinov a certain blindness regarding Meyerhold's work, a defensiveness, an overinsistence upon the originality of his theatrical work as Meyerhold's career came to overshadow his own. Here, Evreinov staged his Symbolist-influenced productions of Schiller's *Maid of Orleans* and D'Annunzio's *Francesca da Rimini*, the former presenting Joan of Arc, played by a man, from the perspective of the medieval mentality and the latter seeking to create a picturesque and evocative rendering of the mood and spirit of the thirteenth century.[26]

These productions, purposely primitive to the point of being childlike in spirit and design and extraordinarily harmonious in execution, anticipated Evreinov's greatest directorial venture into the creative reconstruction of past culture, the Ancient Theatre (Starinny teatr), founded in St. Petersburg in 1907-08 with Baron Nikolai Driezen. In its two seasons of operation, this enterprise crystallized the then current antiquarian trend in scholarship and the arts, and especially the fascination with theatrical forms of the past, their rediscovery and recreation. Although Meyerhold had done earlier experiments in this field, most notably his staging of Maeterlinck's *Sister Beatrice* at Komissarzhevskaya's theatre in 1906, and while the Symbolist poets — Ivanov, Bruisov, Balmont, et al. — underwrote this approach with their theories, no one effort was as sustained, as systematic and ultimately as influential as the Ancient Theatre. The spirit which infused the productions at the Ancient Theatre was fittingly captured in the permanent stage curtain designed by Alexander Benois, representing a tapestry from the thirteenth century, inscribed with favorite medieval motifs. A knight stood at stage left, a maiden petting a unicorn at stage right and the tapestry was parted in three places — by an angel at one side, a demon at the other and by Adam and Eve in the middle. The two "cycles" of productions at the Ancient Theatre, the Medieval (1907-08) and the Spanish Golden Age (1911-12) (a third devoted to the Commedia dell'arte, was planned but unfortunately never realized), were filled with the spirited play and naive wonderment of these cultures.[27]

The productions at the Ancient Theatre represented Evreinov's concept of the theatre in life in action. A medieval town square in the early evening bursting with activity both sacred and profane, morality plays enacted on the steps of a cathedral with an onstage audience in attendance reacting to the events depicted as if they were real. All the while, the stench of the Black Death hovered in the air and half-naked flagellants passed in procession. The audience on the square, caught up in the power of religious ecstasy and angered by the performance it was witnessing, stormed the stage, dissolving the scene which the audience in the auditorium was witnessing in disorder, thus ending the spectacle. In all, the scenes recreated onstage were structured more as event than as conventional drama, coming together and breaking apart rather than formally beginning and ending. There was no real exposition, development or resolution, only a strong but fleeting impression, like time and life itself.[28]

Evreinov's childlike miniature work at the Crooked Mirror Theatre, representing the opposite pole of his directing career, was foreshadowed at the Ancient Theatre by several productions, most notably his staging of Adam de la Halle's *Le Jeu de Robin et Marion* (December 7, 1907). Here broad characterizations, flat and oversized settings, playful music, dance, declamation and mime all mingled in a joyous and deceptively simplehearted presentation.[29]

As with his earlier productions for Komissarzhevskaya's theatre and his later experiements with monodrama and the theatre in life, Evreinov's work at the Ancient Theatre whether pastorale, mystery or moralité, was designed to place the audience inside the theatrical moment and the mental set of the historical epoch it represented. Evreinov called this "the reconstruction of the spectator" and his overall approach to the historical theatrical event "artistic reconstruction." "What was produced," wrote one critic, "was not an exact reproduction of the ancient theatre, but rather something in the nature of a fantasy on the theme of the theatre."[30] It was, in fact, a dramatic argument for the theory of theatre in life, employing the focusing and hypnotic power of monodrama.

In his Ancient Theatre productions as in his later mass spectacle experiment, Evreinov employed a mass protagonist, a crowd acting as one to serve as a conduit into a theatrical event of such size and variegated color that we might otherwise become lost. In the process, actual reality was transformed into something more beautiful and more transcendant. Evreinov did not want to do away with the spectator as part of an elitist concept of theatre for oneself as the critics of his time asserted. In the first place, theatre for oneself was not intended to be elitist, but democratic, flowing into the larger concept of the theatre in life in which we can all become "aristocrats" by choice. Evreinov's multifaceted directorial work in such genres as monodrama, the theatre of marionettes, the showbooth (balagan), ancient theatre, folk rituals, operetta, intermedii, harlequinades and mass spectacles makes it clear that what he was instead trying to do was to so absorb the audience into the theatrical event that it would lose its traditional identity, just as the concept of theatre would itself be transformed.

Throughout his career, Evreinov alternated between serious scholarship and often naive and whimsical theatrical play. These two tendencies were united at the Ancient Theatre, where a scholarly lecture often preceded the evening's theatrical fare. Evreinov was preoccupied with establishing the legitimacy of himself as a serious artist-thinker and the theatre as pre-eminent among the arts and sciences.

Evreinov's more whimsical side was on display in two later Petersburg theatrical ventures, the shortlived Merry Theatre for Grownup Children (Vesely teatr pozheloy detey, 1908-9), co-founded with Fyodor Komissarzhevsky on the premises of his sister's theatre, and especially, the Crooked Mirror Theatre (Teatr "Krivoe zerkalo"), co-founded by editor-critic A. R. Kugel and his actress wife Z. V. Kholmskaya (December 6, 1908), of which Evreinov became the Artistic Director and guiding spirit.

In his six years as the Crooked Mirror's Artistic Director (1910-14, 1916-17), Evreinov was involved in some one hundred plays, directing about eighty, including fourteen of his own, and translating, advising on or composing music for the rest. These ranged from satirical monodrama to harlequinade and other forms of theatrical pantomime, from mock ceremonial conferences to honor an author or theme (an Evreinov invention) to parodies of theatrical forms (including opera, ballet and cinema), from comic variations on serious contemporary philosophical themes and artistic movements to adaptations of ancient and modern classics.[31] Under Evreinov's guidance, the Crooked Mirror was transformed from a late-night cabaret to the leading exemplar of the "theatre of small forms" movement then sweeping the country. Here Evreinov succeeded where Meyerhold had failed. Meyerhold's foray into late-night theatre, the Strand (Lukomore) was eclipsed by the Crooked Mirror on the opening night bill which they shared (December 6, 1908), long before Evreinov even entered upon the scene.[32]

Evreinov's most popular work as a dramatist at this theatre was *The In-*

spector General (premiere December 11, 1912), a parody of the directorial style of Stanislavsky, Craig and Reinhardt, using Gogol's play as its premise and a play-within-a-play format.[33] Evreinov further parodied Stanislavsky in *The Fourth Wall* (premiere December 22, 1915), again employing a play-within-a-play format. Evreinov showed how a Stanislavsky-based director transformed Gounad's opera *Faust* into a somber exercise in behavioristic acting and literal-minded archeological reconstruction (unlike Evreinov's own experiments with artistic reconstruction at the Ancient Theatre). An old actor, cast for his age rather than his talent, coughs and wheezes his way through the roles of both Faust and Mephistopheles, tenor and basso respectively, since we are told, current research has proven that the latter is but the former's alter-ego. We glimpse him only intermittently by candlelight through a small window in a wall which runs the length of the stage. All the while, unsavory street life commands our attention below the window. In the end, the actor downs a chalice of poison, made real by the director for effect, and he dies.[34]

While at the Crooked Mirror, Evreinov developed his ideas on wit and humor which as always were reinforced by diligent research, ranging from philosophy to anthropology. It seems a huge step from this painting in whimsical theatrical miniatures to Evreinov's work on the Soviet mass spectacle, *The Storming of the Winter Palace* (Vziatie zimmego dvortsa, November 7, 1920), which capped his Russian career, and yet it was a logical step, absolutely consistent with his previous theoretical and practical work.

The Revolution had itself illustrated what Evreinov had long argued, that human life is inherently theatrical, and that the border between theatre and life is porous. Furthermore, the exaltation of the masses, the so-called "dictatorship of the proletariat" which the Revolution had sought to achieve, transformed Evreinov's notion that every man can become an aristocrat in the theatre in life into a reality.

At least nine mass spectacles were staged in Petrograd prior to *The Storming of the Winter Palace*. Designed to glorify the proletariat, these spectacles stressed concentration of feeling, action and style, from the use of the crowds as a mass protagonist to the careful orchestration of music, lighting, sound and visual effects, costumes and dialogue which was kept to a minimum.

The Storming of the Winter Palace was presented in Uritsky Square on November 7, 1920 from approximately 10:30 to 12:00 p.m. to commemorate the third anniversary of the October revolution. It engaged some ten thousand performers (with the crowd, estimates run as high as one hundred thousand), including actors, workers, dancers, circus performers and whole sectors of the Red Army and Baltic Fleet. The central action took place on two platforms — the Red, directed by F. S. Viven, N. V. Petrov and N. I. Misheev in a style that combined the historical with the heroic; and the White, directed by A. R. Kugel, K. N. Derzhavin and A. G. Movshenson in comically grotesque fashion.

The action also spilled out onto a bridge connecting the two platforms and onto the square (the third genuinely "historical" stage) as well as into the Winter Palace itself. Here, moments of internal life were glimpsed briefly through the building's fifty windows which functioned like the frames in an unwinding reel of film. Rockets, fireworks, rifle and machine gun fire filled the air, along with the sound of singing, chanting, shouting and the booming guns of the battleship "Aurora," which lay anchored in the Neva. Hugo Varlikh conducted the brass band which accompanied the action. Professor Maizel's lighting effects showcased the set designed by Yuri Annenkov, a series of flats and platforms juxtaposed with the existing architecture on the square.[35]

Visually, the spectacle resembled a medieval mystery seen through the prism of twentieth-century expressionist art. The flats which backed the Red and the White platforms were slanted at sharp, irregular angles. Those on the White platform were off-white, pink and light brown in color. Those on the Red platform were all brick red, representing factory works. Smokestacks popped up amidst the factory walls, which were dotted with rows of windows containing a painted yellow light. Long runs of broad steps led up to both the Red and the White platforms, producing heroic and ludicrous impressions respectively. The Winter Palace was kept free of constructed pieces.

As in his experiments at the Ancient Theatre, Evreinov was here concerned with artistic rather than archeological reconstruction. In depicting the fall of Kerensky's Provisional Government, Evreinov did not hesitate to take certain liberties, mixing the real and the grotesque. The bourgeoisie were dressed in elegant but exaggerated costumes, suggestive of a masquerade ball. Bankers in gold and silver top hats and gigantic carnations straddled huge money bags labelled with the sums that they allegedly contained. They were joined by military men in dress uniforms, cocked hats, white sashes, monocles and medals. This contrasted sharply with the drab uniforms and proletarian dress of those on the Red platform and in the jeeps and trucks which came racing through the arch of the General Staff Headquarters into the square. The dignified comportment of the bourgeoisie likewise contrasted dramatically with scenes of workers trudging up flights of stairs, bent over from the weight of the tools on their backs.

Among both the Red and White contingents, there was great uniformity in movement and gesture, and repetition was used to great effect. Twenty-five "Kerenskys" played by ballet dancers, read a speech three times in succession, while the generals and dignitaries on the White platform applauded after each sentence by slowly and rhythmically tapping hammers.

Similarly, two hundred workers entered onto the opposing platform, hammers in hand, shouting in unison as their stage was bathed in red light. One-half of the workers proceeded to simulate work, while the other half stood in bas-relief and hammers striking anvils provided musical accompaniment. Thirty "Lenins" responded to the exhortations of the crowd by delivering a speech which culminated in one of the frequent repetitions of "The Internationale."[36]

Although somewhat more stylized than Evreinov's productions at the Ancient Theatre, the mass spectacle nevertheless embodied a similar scenic as

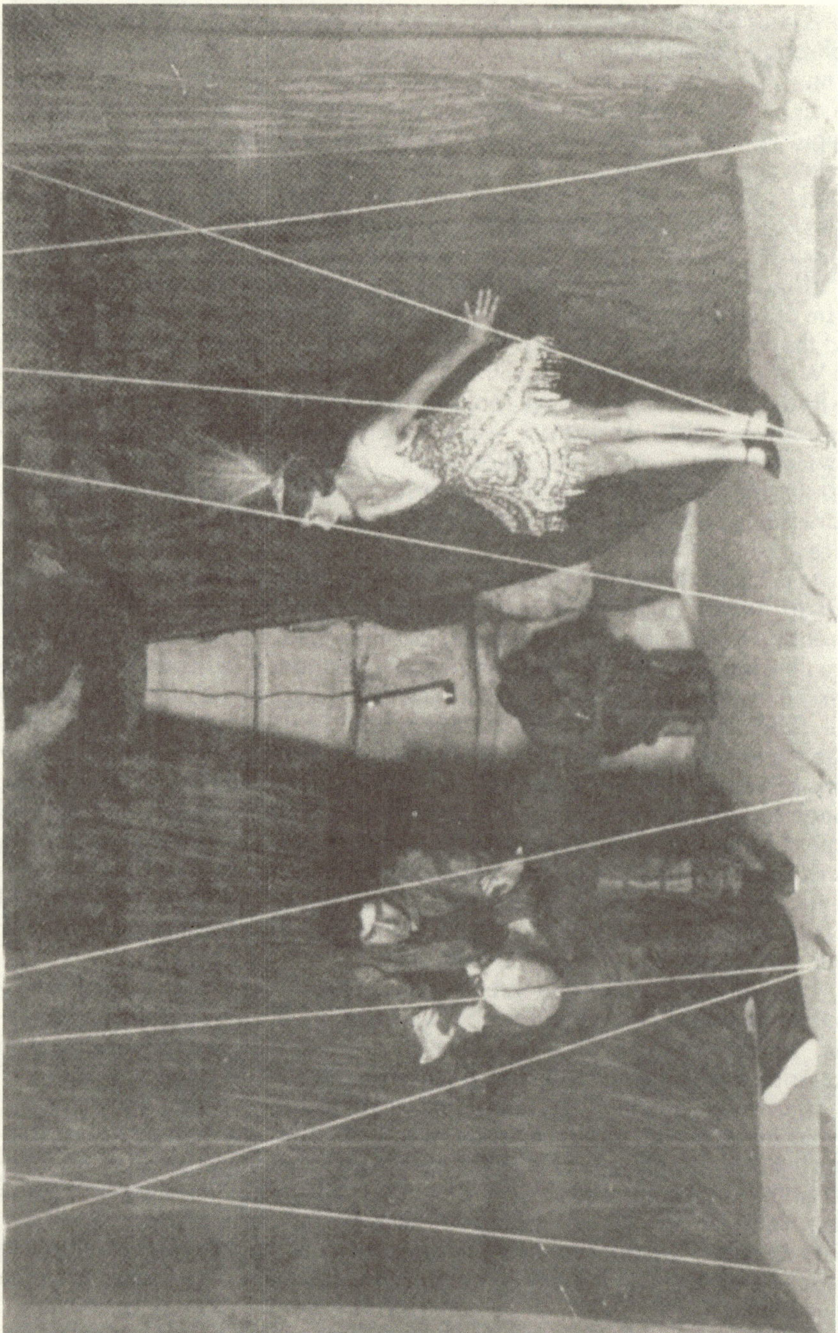

A scene from a 1931 Paris production of Evreinov's *Theatre of the Soul.*

well as spiritual and ideological naivete'. *The Storming of the Winter Palace* depicted the struggle between Good (the Reds) and Evil (the Whites), the expulsion of the Satanic host under the banner of capitalism from the world which the Bolsheviks were working to transform into a proletarian paradise.[37]

Both the medieval productions and the mass spectacles were events designed to re-affirm the beliefs of the already converted. Although the medieval presentations drew upon liturgical drama, while Soviet agit-prop was secular and even anti-religious, each offered theatre in life as consolatory faith to a modern-day audience, a return to shared mystery and communion. The inclusion of actual participants in the original storming of the Winter Palace in Evreinov's commemorative spectacle, made his concept of theatre in life even more palpable. Finally, Evreinov had found a life-size canvas upon which to paint, possessed of a spirituality and cosmic scope borrowed from the Ancient Theatre. And via the use of a mass protagonist, a device he had earlier employed in staging Spanish and medieval drama, Evreinov at least partially realized the principle of monodrama, that is totally involving the audience in the various manifestations of a single "character's" psyche. At the same time, with the mass spectacle, Evreinov moved further than ever toward transcending the concept of character altogether, substituting agents as he had done earlier in his monodrama, *In the Stage-Wings of the Soul*.

Director, dramatist, theorist and would-be philosopher, Evreinov was above all else a provocateur by nature and design. He was practiced in the art of transgression as was the art he championed. Theatre, in his estimation, absorbed all other arts. His own nondramaturgical writings, sometimes printed in red ink and accompanied by suggested trumpet blasts and other quasi-theatrical effects, boldly assaulted the reader and proclaimed themselves to be theatre of the printed page.[38]

Evreinov loved and admired those artists, such as Beardsley and Rops whose theatricality stemmed from a talent for "artistic scandal," who provoked and transgressed, finding beauty in the ripeness of sin:

> *. . . the justification of vice through beauty; the ornamentation of sin beyond aesthetic recognition; the transformation of the Black God into the White God who represents the highest magic of art.*[39]

Art without borders; life without limits. Art into life and life into art. The power and the possibilities were endless.

Symptomatic of both his own talent for artistic scandal and the hidden realms to which his art aspired was Evreinov's championing of nudity on the stage, a position far from popular in his own day. Unlike nakedness which Evreinov maintained never breaks through "the problem of sexuality," nudity requires "sharpness of outline, a discriminating look in the eyes, chasteness of pose and gesture, the absence of underscoring and innocence of action." It suggests more than it is and represented for Evreinov a symbol of revelation.[40]

Through the phenomenal realm of the body we may hope to perceive the noumenal realm of the soul. Like the eternal Self in *In the Stage-Wings of the Soul*, who transcended the physical Self and the related trauma of socio-sexual experiences on his way to some noumenal bliss, Evreinov was arguing for the gradual revelation of essence through form. This recalls Evreinov's fascination with and adoption of the commedia mask, itself an essence captured in a seemingly primitive form. As a subscriber to the Bergsonian theory of creative evolution, Evreinov believed that man must keep evolving his form until it reveals his god-like essence. Evreinov conceived of this process in theatrical terms. He redefined man as an animal who plays and through play, the transformation of internal and external reality, transforms and ennobles himself.

Evreinov could no more tolerate a veiled woman than he could a curtained stage, anything which kept form apart from essence, appearance masking truth. He could justify his own mask by the end he was seeking to serve — true revelation. He sought to put himself and his audience in another place entirely, whether it was a medieval town square, or inside a man's body. It was essential that his audience not just bear witness to an event. They must live it, be in the event and of the event, to break through the form of the spectacle in search of essence. Theatre was shamanistic for Evreinov, the means by which man might discover his own godhead. This was real magic, and not the mere aesthetic sleight of hand with which Evreinov is usually credited. In fact, Evreinov spent the last ten years of his life working on a book entitled, *The Revelation of Art* (Otkrovenie iskusstva), begun in 1934 but left unfinished at his death, in which he sought once and for all to examine and define the power of suggestion or "magic" of art.[41]

Evreinov said of the religious painter Nesterov that "his focus is not on God but on man. He loves man and believes in his salvation."[42] So it was with Evreinov. He believed, as did Oscar Wilde, that man is saved by the "beautiful lie," which is theatre, the will to transform and be transformed. Evreinov, an atheist, worshipped the god "Theatrarch," which was in a sense yet another mask for Evreinov himself to hide behind. Unlike Artaud and the Absurdists whose vision presumed a god who was either indifferent or else cruel and savage, Evreinov's benign theatrical divinity would dispel the chaos of modern times via white magic.

It should by now be evident that the lightmindedness of which Evreinov was accused was more a matter of style than substance. His ironic posturings were designed to mask a certain romantic idealism, an optimistic view of mankind to which he was never completely reconciled.

As with any artist whose work is both broad in scope and noble in intention, it is easy to claim too much in Evreinov's behalf. The questions of originality and causality in the realm of art, which so preoccupied Evreinov during his lifetime, need not concern us here. The history of art is not, after all, a court of law. Evreinov's career and accomplishments should speak directly to a society like our own which has itself passed through a decade of romantic idealism, only to be victimized by the cult of personality and a confused value system which has helped plunge us into a state of almost total self-absorption. We have walked the tightrope between self-realization and self-advertisement. We have searched for essences and become mired in forms which have become fragmented, mixed and shrunken in size. We have mythologized the common man and even the household object, made royalty of our celebrities and destroyed our heroes. Our constant search for new faiths has resulted in an endless variety of readily disposable fads. And we have the theatre that we deserve, not the one we need. We seem for the moment to have lost our capacity to dream.

Evreinov, the retrospective dreamer, sifted through history in search of the philosopher's stone. But his intense efforts to seize and penetrate the historical moment, to discover its essence, seem distinctly modern. Evreinov examined what was for him the central historical conflict between man's need for community and his desire for individuation, a struggle clearly embodied in Evreinov's own life and work.

To the extent that Evreinov sought to swallow the world, to subjugate it to the force of his personality, history punished him by withholding his full measure of fame. History distrusts a paradox and so sentenced Evreinov to watch in self-imposed exile while other Russian artists of his generation were acclaimed the great innovators of their day and still others, such as Pirandello and Artaud, whose ideas he prefigured, surpassed him in reputation. History has treated Evreinov with an irony, which despite his wit and good humor, he never could learn to appreciate. It is time to give him his due.

NOTES

[1]A. A. Mgebrov, *Žizn' v teatre*, vol. 2 (Moskva-Leningrad: Academia, 1932], p. 312.

[2]N. N. Evreinov, *Teatr kak takovoj* (St. Petersburg: Sovremennoe iskusstvo, 1912).

[3]N. N. Evreinov, *The Main Thing*, in *Life as Theatre: Five Modern Plays, trans. and ed. by Christopher Collins (Ann Arbor: Ardis Publishers, 1973), p. 177.*

[4]*B. V. Kazanskij, Metod teatra* (Analiz sistemy N. N. Evreinova) (Leningrad: "Academia," 1925) pp. 26 and 52; N. N. Evreinov, "O nekotoryx xodjačix terminax (k pereizdaniju *Teatra kak takavogo*)" *Žizn' iskusstva 44 (November 5, 1922):6.*

[5]*A. R. Kugel', "Teatral'nye zametki," Teatr i iskusstvo* 39 (September 25, 1911): 726-28; Evg. Bezpjatov, *Ežegodnik Imperatorskix teatrov* (March 1909): 75-81; D. Filosov, "Teatr i muzyka," *Naša gazeta*, p. 6.

[6]B. Glagolin, "Russkij argonavt," *Žurnal teatra Literaturno-xudožestvennogo obščestva* 1 (1909-10), pp. 19-20.

[7]Evg. Znosko-Borovskij, *Russkij teatr načala XX veka* (Prague: Plamja, 1925), p. 320.

[8]N. N. Evreinov, "O satiričeskoj monodrame i ispol'zovanii ee na scene 'Krivogo zerkala,' " "V škole ostroumija," pp. 6-7, 13-14; N. N. Evreinov, "K postanovke *Gore ot uma* A. S. Griboedova (1935)," CGALI SSSR, fond no. 982, ed. xr. no. 38, opis' no. 1, pp. 9-12.

[9]Martin Esslin, *The Theatre of the Absurd*, 2nd ed. (Garden City, N.Y.: Doubleday and Co.; 1969), pp. 43-44.

[10]N. N. Evreinov, "O satiričeskoj monodrame. . .," p. 23.

[11]Petr Ju, "Krivoe zerkalo," *Teatr i iskusstvo 43 (October 21, 1912), p. 817.*

[12]*N. N. Evreinov, The Theatre of the Soul*, in *Life as Theatre: Five Modern Plays*, trans. and ed. by Christopher Collins (Ann Arbor: Ardis Publishers, 1973), p. 29.

[13]*Ibid.*, pp. 29-30.

[14]Interview with A. A. Kašina-Evreinova, Paris, France, June, 1976.

[15]N. N. Evreinov, *Teatr dlja sebja. Čast' pervaja* (Petrograd: Sovremennoe iskussstvo, 1915), p. 77.

[16]*Ibid.*, pp. 68, 86-88, 90-91, 109, 148, 159, 174; N. N. Evreinov, *Tajna Rasputina* o mifologičeskoj maske) (Petrograd: Byloe, 1924), pp. 49, 58-60, 75; N. N. Evreinov, *Rops.*

Kritičeskij očerk (St. Petersburg: Sovremennoe iskusstvo, 1910), p. 57; N. N. Evreinov, *Nesterov. Očerk* Petrograd: Tret'ja straža, 1922), pp. 56 and 79.

[17]N. N. Evreinov, *Teatr dlja sebja. Čast' vtoraja* (Petrograd: Sovremennoe iskusstvo, 1916), pp. 31, 33-36; Evreinov, *Teatr dlja sebja. Čast' pervaja*, pp. 40-42; N. N. Evreinov, *The Theatre in Life*, trans. and ed. by Alexander I. Nazaroff (London: George G. Harrap and Co., 1927), pp. 35-37, 42.

[18]*Evreinov, Tajna Rasputina*, pp. 49, 58-60, 75; Evreinov, *Teatr dlja sebja. Čast' pervaja, pp. 68, 109, 148, 159, 174.*

[19]*Evreinov, Teatr dlja sebja. Čast' pervaja*, pp. 58-59.

[20]All information relating to "The Theatre and the Scaffold" (Teatr i ešafot) comes from the A. A. Baxrušin State Central Theatrical Museum (Gosudarstvennyj central'nyj teatral'nyj muzej imeni A. A. Baxrušina), fond no. 96 (Evreinov, N. N.), no. postuplenija 192.161-192.162, "Teatre i ešafot (materialy, zametiki, vyreszki)." Among his notes for "The Theatre and the Scaffold," Evreinov has written in, "Monodrama — co-experiencing with the sacrifice"; N. N. Evreinov, "K poznaniju teatral'noj parodii," "V škole ostoumija, O teatre 'Krivoe zerkalo,'" CGALI SSSR, fond no. 982, opis' no. 1, ed.xr. no. 9, p. 53; N. N. Evreinov, *Azazel i Dionis. O proisxoždenii sceny v svjazi s začatkami dramy u semitov* (Leningrad: Academia, 1924), pp. 13, 16, 46, 65, 67, 95-6, 105-6, 156 and 190; N. N. Evreinov, *Pervobytnaja drama germancev* (Iz pra-istorii teatra germano-skandinavskix narodov) (Petrograd: Poljarnaja zvezda. 1922), pp. 5 and 8.

[21]Evreinov, *Teatr dlja sebja. Čast' pervaja*, pp. 114-15.

[22]N. N. Evreinov, *Pro Scena Sua* (Petrograd: Prometej, 1914), pp. 25-26, 36-37.

[23]Evreinov, *Teatr kak takovoj*, p. 77.

[24]Premiered February 20, 1921 at the Theatre of Free Comedy (Teatr "Vol'noj komedii") under the direction of Nikolai Petrov with designs by Evreinov's frequent associate Jurij Annenkov. Nikolai Petrov, *50 i 500* (Moskva: Vserossiyskoe Teatral'noe obščestvo, 1960), p. 209.

[25]Evreinov, *The Main Thing*, pp. 67-8; Collins, "Nikolai Evreinov as Playwright," in *Life as Theatre: Five Modern Plays*, pp. xx-xxi.

[26]Edward Stark, "Recenzija *Francesca da Rimini*," *Teatr i iskusstvo* 17 (April 28, 1913), pp. 376-77; Kn. Sergej Volkonskij, *Otkliki teatra* (Petrograd, 1914), pp. 20-22; A. R. Kugel', "Recenzija: *Francesca da Rimini*," Novaja Rus' 52 (October 6, 1908), pp. 3-4; Smolenskij, "Okolo rampy: teatr g-zi Komissarževskoj — *Francesca da Rimini* G. D'Annunzio," *Birževye vedomosti* 10743 (October 6, 1908), p. 4; B. T. "*Francesca da Rimini* na scene teatra Komissarževskoj (Beseda s. N. N. Evreinovym)," *Rannee utro* 236 (August 30, 1908), p. 4; "Staryj drug," "Vtoraja *Francesca*," *Teatr* 259 (September 6, 1908), pp. 3-7.

[27]Edward Stark. *Starinnyj teatr* (St. Petersburg: Tret'ja straža, 1922), pp. 5-9, 15; Viktorija Čekan, "Starinnyj teatr: Ispanskij cikl, Evreinov-Driezen," *Žizn' iskusstva* 21 (May 29, 1922), p. 4.

[28]N. N. Evreinov, *Jarmarka na indikt sv. Denisa* in *Dramatičeskie sočinenija*, vol. 2 (St. Petersburg: Sovremennoe iskusstvo, 1914), quoted in (and translated by) Christopher Moody, "The Ancient Theatre in St. Petersburg 1907-08 and 1911-12," p. 23; Stark, *Starinnyj teatr, pp. 15-18.*

[29]*Stark, Starinnyj teatr*, pp. 24-27.

[30]Kazanskij, *Metod teatra*, p. 103; Igor' Grabar', "Teatr i xudožniki," *Vesy* 4 (1908), p. 95.

[31]For a complete listing of all productions staged by Evreinov at the Crooked Mirror Theatre, as well as all of the programmes that premiered during his tenure as Artistic Director, see my dissertation "The Monodrama of Nikolaj Evreinov," University of Kansas, 1977. My information is derived from Evreinov's unpublished memoirs, "In the School of Wit. About the 'Crooked Mirror' Theatre and My Many Years of Work There as Dramatist and Chief Artistic Director," (V škole ostroumija. O teatre 'Krivoe zerkalo' i moej mnogoletnej rabote v nem, kak dramaturga i glavnogo režissera." Central'nyj gosudarstvennyj arxiv literatury i iskusstva SSSR. Fond no. 982. Opis' no. 1 ed. xr. nos. 4, 9, 10, 12, 13.

[32]Nikolaj Volkov, *Mejerxol'd*, vol. 2 (Moskva-Leningrad: Academia, 1929), pp. 37-39; G. Kryžickij, "Vospominanija. Laboratorija smexa'," *Teatr* 8 (August 1967), pp. 110-11; Kugel', *List'ja s dereva*, p. 198; Xolmskaja, "Krivoe zerkalo," p. 53. Evreinov ascribed the failure of the Strand to Mejerxol'd's belief that theatre is born of literature. The Strand, in Evreinov's opinion, embodied this idea. Evreinov was fond of reiterating this, because he claimed that

following the publication of his "Apology for Theatricality" (Apologija teatral'nosti, 1908) and *The Theatre as Such* (Teatr kak takovoj, 1912), Mejerxol'd reversed his position.

[33]It is interesting to note that Evrienov did not choose to parody the directorial work of Mejerxol'd. If Evreinov were really selecting people whom he wanted to debunk, Mejerxol'd would most certainly have been first on his list. But such was not the object of this particular exercise. The directors whose work was parodied were recognized by Evreinov as being major forces in the contemporary theatre. To include Mejerxol'd in this company, even as an object of ridicule, would have been an acknowledgement of his importance as a moving force in contemporary theatre. Although Evreinov poked fun at these directors for their stylistic excesses, he was using them as evidence in his argument for the right of the director to be the author of the stage production.

Evreinov's cordial relationship with Stanislavskij was ended as a result of this parody. He claimed that Stanislavskij felt compelled to re-stage *The Inspector General* at MXAT as a result of this parody treatment of his original staging, which featured actors sitting with their backs to the audience in the worst "fourth wall" tradition and a barrage of auditory and visual effects which obscured the main action of the play. Evreinov also credited his concept of theatricality, set forth in *The Theatre as Such*, with influencing Stanislavskij to redo his production. Evreinov later qualified this, saying that it was Evgenij Vaxtangov's productions of *Princess Turandot* and *Erik XIV* which so influenced Stanislavskij. Of course, said Evreinov, it was *he* who had influenced Vaxtangov. N. N. Evreinov, *Revizor* in *Dramatičeskie sočinenija* vol. 3 (p'esy iz repertuara Krivogo zerkala) (Petrograd: Academia, 1923; N. N Evreinov, "O nekotoryx xodjači terminax (K pereizdaniju *Teatr kak takovoj*)", Žizn' iskusstva 44 (November 5, 1922), p. 6; Evreinov, "V gostjax u carja Nikolaja II-go," p. 40; N. N Evreinov, "K pereocenke teatral'nosti (Okončanie)," *Žizn' iskusstva* 38 (September 25, 1923), pp. 11-12.

[34]N. N. Evreinov, *The Fourth Wall*, trans. by Burke (unpublished). The original was unavailable.

[35]N. N. Evreinov, "Vzjatie Zimnego dvorca," *Žizn' iskusstva 596-97 (October 30 and 31, 1920), p. 1; "Inscenirovka 'Vzjatie Zimnego dvorca na ploščadi tov. Urickogo, 8-go nojabrja 1920 goda," Manuscript Division of the Leningrad State Theatrical Museum; Jurij Annenkov, Dnevnik moix vstreč. Cikl tragedii*, vol. 2 (New York: Inter-Language Literary Associates, 1966), pp. 120, 122; N. Šubskij, "Na ploščadi Urickogo: Vpečatlenija moskviča," Manuscript Division of the Leningrad State Theatrical Museum; V. G. Samojlov, "Revoljucionnye prazdnestva," in *Teatral'noe dekoracionnoe iskusstvo v SSSR (Leningrad, 1927), pp. 188-89, 193.*

[36]*Information derived from production photographs, Annenkov's sketches of the set, and various written breakdowns of the scenario for the spectacle in the Manuscript Division of the Leningrad State Theatrical Museum.*

[37]*Huntly Carter, The New Spirit in the Russian Theatre 1917-28* (London: Brentano's, 1921), pp. 144-45.

[38]See *The Theatre as Such (Teatr kak takovoj).*

[39]*N. N. Evreinov, Beardsley, Kriticeskij ocerk* (St. Petersburg: Sovremennoe iskusstvo, 1912), p. 31.

[40]This article was later included in an anthology edited by Evreinov entitled *Nudity on the Stage* (Nagota na scené) (St. Petersburg: Novoe vremja, 1911); *Evreinov, Nagota na scene*, pp. 42-44.

[41]N. N. Evreinov, "Otkrovenie iskusstva." The Russian Archives, Columbia University, EVR. A. A. 26-1, K-6. 6.22.

[42]Kazanskij, *Metod teatra* (Analiz sistemy N. N. Evreinova), p. 80.

Arrival upon the whaling ground. "There she blows!" Plates from *Life in the South Seas* by Capt. E. C. Williams (New York: Polhemus and DeVries, 1860). Courtesy of Charles F. Batchelder.

Whale Oil & Greasepaint: On Tour With Benjamin Russell & E. C. Williams

JOHN MARSH

Of all the panoramic fare that bid for the attention of nineteenth century audiences, none had more appeal than two panoramas of American whaling which grew out of the experience of those sometime whalemen, Benjamin Russell and E. C. Williams, who barnstormed mid nineteenth century America as the exhibitors and delineators of panoramas of South Sea whaling voyages. Audiences about the country were captivated not only by the painted spectacle passing slowly before their eyes of the pursuit, the encounter and the death struggles of the monsters of the deep, but by the exhibitor's monologue which imaged not a little of whaling's techniques and skills, its dangers and thrills, its architectonics and its economics. But beyond the accurately rendered details of a whaling voyage and of a then vital industry, there was the full panoply of South Sea adventure — especially pleasing to the palates of nineteenth century romantics: exotic ports of call like Pitcairn's Island, the Marquesas or Nuku Hiva; or native dances, huts, temples, canoes. It was magnificent entertainment of its kind, and something of the story comes through in the surviving promotional materials and in the pages of the popular press of the day whose reviewers came, saw and were captivated.[1]

The earlier of the two panoramas, Russell's "A Whaling Voyage Round the World," commenced exhibition after two years of "studious" preparation at Fair Haven and New Bedford in December 1848. At the New Bedford showing Captain Daniel McKenzie, described as the "exhibitor," carried the audience "along through the various scenes, all of which he has visited, interspersing his descriptions with anecdotes and narratives, which enhance the entertainment very much."[2] These devolved, no doubt, from the captain's own career as a whaling master from 1818-1846, during which period he made eight voyages to the Pacific. An entertaining and colorful character, not at all averse to public appearances, McKenzie, then the Weigher and Gauger of the New Bedford Customs House, was an ideal choice to launch successfully a panoramic venture.

The apex of the tour that followed New Bedford was undoubtedly Boston to which the panorama came early in January 1849. The handbill for its showing at Amory Hall announced performances every evening and Wednesday and Saturday afternoons at 3 o'clock.[3] Advertisements and reviews in the press of the day tell as much of the story as we are likely to

John L. Marsh is Professor of English in the Department of English and Theatre Arts at Edinboro State College, Pennsylvania.

know. The *Boston Post,* for instance, was rhapsodic, calling the panorama "original and diversified in its details, accurate in its delineations, and beautiful in its execution" — particularly the "spirit-stirring whaling scenes."[4] After enumerating the succession of whaling views, the *Post's* reviewer concluded by lauding the panorama's originality of design and matchlessness of execution: "Everybody must go and see it, for we assure them it is, without exaggeration, a production of surpassing excellence."

The *Boston Atlas* was no less enthusiastic, claiming that no evening could be spent in a more interesting manner: "It is one of those very few exhibitions, the reality of which surpasses our expectations."[5] The paper's correspondent noted the panorama's appeal to those who had visited the scenes in question; in them it must produce "vivid reminiscenses." Those not so fortunate, he maintained, had now the opportunity to make the voyage vicariously. Caught up in the spell of what he had witnessed, his prose turned purplish: "Bays, beautiful and calm as summer skies, dotted with verdant spots; islands whose rocky and precipitous peaks pierce the heavens, or whose soft green foliage denotes the regions of the equator" — and so forth.

In reviewing "A Whaling Voyage Round the World," *The Boston Evening Transcript* echoed the tone of the *Post* and *Atlas,* calling it "something at once interesting, instructive and unique."[6] There followed what amounted to a summary of the program with fully orchestrated references to local color — "all the loveliness of their scenery [islands of the Pacific,] all the luxuriance of their vegetation, all the singularly [sic singularity] and picturesqueness of their costume." The paper's correspondent concluded his review by observing that the panorama's accuracy was "vouched for" by those who had visited the scenes it presented. That audiences were essentially in agreement with the complementary points of view expressed by the press would seem indicated by Russell's five month run in Boston.[7]

Probably the city by city perambulations of "A Voyage" are lost beyond recall, but what has come to light in the way of advertisements and reviews suggests not a few of the promotional gambits and something of the showmanship that contributed to the generally favorable reception Russell's canvas enjoyed. The ad, for instance, that announced the Buffalo, New York, showing late in November and early December 1849 is instructive:

> *Unparalled Attraction!*
> *WHALING VOYAGE ROUND THE WORLD!*
> *Russell's*
> *GRAND, ORIGINAL AND EXCITING*
> *MOVING PANORAMA!!*
> *Will be opened on MONDAY NEXT;* ***for a few evenings only,*** *at* ***CLINTON HALL,*** *corner of Washington and Clinton Streets.*
>
> *This truly wonderful and magnificent triumph of Art, from Original Drawings taken from life by BENJAMIN RUSSELL, the labor of about five years, covering near three miles of canvass, the largest Painting ever presented, giving graphic views of the*

city of New Bedford, the Western and Cape de Verde Islands, city of Rio Janeiro, Cape Horn, Island of Robinson Cruso, Pitcairn, Marquesas, Society and Sandwich Islands — a great variety of Whaling Adventures, Cape of Good Hope, and closing at the renowned island of St. Helena.

Doors open at 7 — commences moving at half-past 7. Admission 25 cents.

There will be an exhibition on SATURDAY AFTERNOON at 3 o'clock, for the accommodation of the children in the schools, and for those who are unable to attend in the evening.[8]

Typically the panoramist has not undervalued his product. It is "GRAND, ORIGINAL AND EXCITING"; the exhibition itself is "UNPARALLELED." The two years in the making alluded to in the Boston handbill has become "the labor of about five years" and nowhere does Purrington's name appear as sharing in the creation of "the largest Painting ever presented." New Englanders had been attracted presumably by Russell's references to whaling scenes but these are down-played for the residents of Buffalo, whose attention is called rather to the panorama's exotic ports of call. The closing lines with their reference to special Saturday showings for the accommodation of school children illustrate the efforts of the promoter to tap every possible interest group.

Within a week of its Buffalo closing, Russell's panorama was in Cleveland, Ohio, at Empire Hall, one of the city's most desirable exhibition sites.[9] Ads in the local papers from 8 December to 15 December 1849, emphasize (as they had in Buffalo) the geographical knowledge to be obtained and specify that Russell's voyage occupied less than two hours.[10] Purrington's name is again coupled with Russell's and something of the past reception of the panorama is noted which not so subtly implies that what was good enough for eastern cities ought to be very good indeed for Cleveland:

This Panorama has been exhibited in Boston, New Bedford, Nantucket, and other Eastern Cities, during the past year, and has been pronounced by thousands who are familiar with the scenes it represents, to be a most faithful and characteristic delineation. In New Bedford, where it was originally exhibited, many of the views were received with shouts of applause by those who had long retired from the sea, but who had been familiar with them in early life. The great attractions which this Painting offers to the beholder, cannot fail to ensure a full attendance.[11]

Cincinnati evidently was next on Russell's itinerary, for the panorama was advertised throughout the holiday season of 1849 at Apollo Hall in that city.[12] The text of a continuing ad harkens to the testimony of "Old Whaling Captains" to the accuracy of Russell's views, based as they were on "actual observation."[13] One newspaper notice, in particular, refers to that epical Boston showing: "The elite of the city visited it by the thousands, and it comes before us with the most unquestionable testimony of its truthfulness."[14] And finally a typical advertisement in the Cincinnati press makes much of the panorama's informational and educational value, calling attention to a special afternoon showing for children: "It is a very instructive lesson, especially to boys, who will gain much useful information in regard to whaling, &c."[15]

Showings to special groups were a recurring phenomenon, and in Pittsburgh, Pennsylvania, "at the request of many of their own number" there was a special showing on the panorama's final night for that city's "colored population."[16] In Louisville, Kentucky, too, special exhibitions were advertised such as an afternoon and evening showing for ladies.[17] In Louisville where the panorama opened on 18 March 1850 Russell, specifically mentioned as the delineator, is said to explain the various scenes and relate many interesting matters in connection with them.[18] The final Louisville ad emphasizes as had those in Buffalo and Cleveland the geographical wonders to be observed: "The Azores, the Cape de Ver Islands, Rio Janeiro, Cape Horn, Pitcairn Island, the Society Islands, and other islands . . . together with a vast variety of sea scenery, the capture of whales, storms, etc."[19]

The St. Louis, Missouri, showing, which evidently followed that in Louisville, appears notable only in that the admission charge appears as 50 cents rather than the usual 25 cents. Announcements ran in the local papers from 13 to 19 April 1850, locating Russell at yet another Apollo Hall.[20] A brief review in *The Missouri Republican* seems cribbed from materials that had appeared in the Louisville papers: perhaps Russell himself supplied the copy to the paper's obliging reviewer.[21]

Following the St. Louis showing, the panorama drops from sight and no showing is known to this author until that in Baltimore, Maryland, in February and March 1851. There a notice in the *American and Commercial Daily Advertiser* calls attention to the panorama's presence at the Law Buildings and notes that this "unrivaled work of art" has been exhibited in many northern and western cities.[22] Tickets at 25 cents each, children half price, could be obtained at several of the book stores and hotels in the city. A most interesting item in the same paper calls attention to a special showing on March 17 for the benefit of "the widows and families of Capt. JOHN HOLLINGSHEAD and LEYPOLD SALIGMAN, late members of Warren Lodge, free and accepted masons, who were lost in the burning of the steamer Columbus, on the 28th of November last."

The last exhibition of Russell's panorama of which this writer has any knowledge occurred in New York City in September 1851 at Panorama Hall, 398 Broadway. The text of the notice in *The New York Evening Mirror* restores the primacy of the whaling scenes as the principal focus of interest and restates for New York readers the success the panorama achieved in its five-month Boston engagement, which apparently was the measure by which all other showings were gauged.[23] It is possible at this point that Russell tired of the arduous trouping that was unavoidably involved in panoramic exhibitions or that he sensed the freshness and the appeal of his work was now exhausted.

Certainly the 1850s in America were the golden day of panoramas; audiences demanded and got a literal torrent of novelties. George Odell in his monumental *Annals of the New York Stage* gives some indication of the bewildering array of panoramas that clamored for attention: there were voyages to California and Europe; moving pictures of the River Rhine, the Mediterranean and Palestine; "grand" depictions of Ireland or the Hudson River; spectacular evocations of the wars in Hungary and Upper Italy; Scott's campaigns in Mexico; the Battle of Bunker Hill and the Destruction of Charleston; and panoramic treatments of *Pilgrim's Progress* and *Uncle Tom's Cabin*.[24] One can only conclude with Odell that the panorama's claims on the public were "inexhaustible." And in the midst of all this frenzy, it is no wonder that Russell's whaling voyage was lost to sight.

However, within some seven years another whaling panorama bid for the attention of New York audiences. This was Captain E. C. Williams' "South Sea Whaling Vogage," which Odell finds playing in Brooklyn and New York's Williamsburgh section in May and June 1858.[25] About this long-lost panorama and its promoter the only known sources are surviving playbills and the pamphlets printed to accompany the presentation together with reviews and advertisements in the press of the day. The latter, for instance, place Williams' panorama in Massachusetts following its New York area showing and the commentary in the papers of Fall River and New Bedford makes much of a special Fall River showing for school children on 24 September 1858.[26]

The city hall, where it took place, was crowded with some 900 children, and as the hour approached the children's excitement increased. Then as the curtain rose on a map of the whaling grounds, Captain Williams appeared before the audience. Quickly he pointed out the course taken by the whaler from Nantucket to the whaling grounds, and when he concluded, the curtain dropped. When it rose again, in a minute or two, Nantucket was in sight and the panoramic portion of the presentation got underway. Williams asked the children to name various objects as they passed before the eye, a technique which served only to increase the children's excitement to the point where Williams was obliged to pause and restore order. Subsequently, "the children were less boisterous in the expression of their gratification, though occasionally they could hardly be restrained, when something very striking presented itself to their eyes."

The program, so the press maintained, fully described the scenes, and all the scenes mentioned in it were presented. Commenting on the quality of Williams' offering, Fall River's reviewer recorded what he professed to be the general opinion, namely that the paintings were "life-like and well colored" and that the verbal descriptions were "vivid": "the Captain entering into the spirit of the scenes, making the audience feel that they were with him catching whales." At the evening showing that followed the children's matinee the house numbered 500 to 600, and the attendance continued strong throughout the five-day exhibition, the panorama being visited by nearly 5,000 viewers.

Good turnouts were again the story at New Bedford's Liberty Hall, and

MELODEON!

BRILLIANT SUCCESS!

FIFTH WEEK OF

CAPT. E. C. WILLIAMS'

Celebrated Representation of a

SOUTH SEA

WHALING VOYAGE

EXHIBITING AS ABOVE,

EVERY EVENING DURING THE WEEK.

Also, each Wednesday and Saturday Afternoon until further notice.

The Ladies and Children are sure to come.

This thrilling description has received the unqualified praise of the *Press and Public*, wherever it has been exhibited throughout the country, and should not be confounded with other Exhibitions, as this is its First introduction to this City. It has only to be seen to be appreciated.

CAPT. WILLIAMS has followed the sea as Cabin Boy, Mate and Captain, through all the various grades, for nearly Thirty Years, and his description of "Life on the Ocean Wave," every evening, is so truthful, combined with the

BEAUTIFUL SCENERY.

As to elicit the warmest approbation from all.

THE THRILLING

BOAT SCENE!

MANNED BY A FULL CREW!

In a Boat which has made Two Whaling Voyages, will be described from actual life, each evening, shewing the manner of Catching the Whales, Rowing, Darting, Paddling, &c., &c.

Appropriate music in connection with the scenery each evening, by MISS MURDOCK and PROF. FERNALD

The Piano Forte used is from the celebrated Factory of CHICKERING & SONS.

PROGRAMME OF THE VOYAGE.

FIRST SECTION.

PART I.

CHART—Exceedingly interesting and instructive, upon which are laid down the courses and distances sailed and the places touched at by whale ships generally; the feeding-grounds of the Sperm Whale and the wonderful polar and ocean currents. The effect of the latter thoroughly explained in producing the migratory habits of the whale, roaming as he does from sea to sea in quest of food.

PART II.

BRANT POINT LIGHT HOUSE, Nantucket Harbor; Whale ship under repairs; Town of Nantucket; Churches, schools, &c; Wharves and shipping; Fishing boats.

Sailing out of the Harbor; Great Point Light House; Steamer Island Home; Open sea; Clipper ship Sovereign of the Seas, contrasted with the

Whale Ship Maria, of New Bedford, the oldest ship in the United States. Fishing boats, ships, &c.

WESTERN ISLANDS.

PEAK OF PICO.

FAYAL—Go on shore; Beautiful ramble.

Ship in a Squall—Boat adrift, bottom up; Three men overboard; Great loss of ship stores; Perilous situation; The rescue.

School of Porpoises—Fine open sea-views.

CAPE VERDS.

PORT A PRAYA—School of Flying-fish.

PIRATICAL SCHOONER—The chase; The escape.

Glorious Sunset Scene—Portion of a wreck.

PART III.

CROSSING THE LINE—Neptune and Amphitrite, Surgeon, Barber, and assistant; Neptune's court; Sea Nymphs surrounding the Goddess; Initiation, shaving, ducking, &c.

SHIP ON FIRE—Ship in the distance running down; Launching boats; Crew and passengers escaping; Moonlight scene.

RIO JANEIRO—Sugar Loaf Mountain; Town of Rio; Sail around the bay.

At Sea, bound for Cape Horn—Towering Peaks of the Cape; Heavy squall; Torn sails; More moderate weather; Gale increases; Hurricane; Ship hove to; Snow-storm; Ship beating to windward of ice; Innumerable icebergs; Seal in abundance; Aurora Australis; South Pacific Ocean.

JUAN FERNANDEZ.

VALPARAISO—Bay and Town; Men of war, merchant ships, boats, fishermen, &c.

Exhibition of the various implements used in the capture of the Leviathan, such as lines, harpoons, lances, spades, harpoons that have taken whales; also, broken one taken from a whale after being 2 years buried in its flesh; jaw and fin bones; whale and killer's teeth; barnacles, &c.

SECOND SECTION.

During this section the **Celebrated and Thrilling Boat Scene**, with its **Life-like Representations**, acknowledged by all who have seen it as **True to Nature**.

WHALE SHIP ON THE CRUISING GROUNDS—Men at the mast-heads; Whale discovered; There she blows!

School of Sperm Whales—Lower the boats! Lower away!

English Boats in Sight—Head and head; The exciting race, Yankees victorious.

Dart!—We're fast! we're fast! Stern all, for your lives! Clear away that lance! Wet line, wet line! Hold on line! Slack, slack! Do you mean to carry the boat under! Pull ahead, now. Lie, lie, lie! Now then! Lay me on, I tell you! agony intense!

Dying Convulsions—The unspeakable flurry; The death.

Towing Dead Whale to the Ship, with all four boats.

Cutting in the Whale—Whale ship's decks; Sharks and birds innumerable; The blanket piece; Boiling out the oil; All hands at work.

Floating Carcase—Mistaken for rocks.

TOMBEZ—Peruvian river, &c.; Boats towing raft of water casks; Alligators; South American Tigers; Alligator attacked; Men put to flight.

At Sea Again—Whale craunching up boat; Men jumping overboard; Boats springing for the scene of disaster.

Whale rushing along 15 to 20 miles an hour, with man on his jaw, suspended to his teeth.

The Whaleman's Dream—Man on Whale's back; Whale running furiously.

FEJEE ISLANDS—Chiefs' war canoes; Savages, Deserter from the ship held by the savages; 20 lbs. powder as ransom; Sand for powder; Deserter dragged to the boat; The discovery of the sand; The pursuit and narrow escape.

Tremendous Conflict between a Whale, Thrasher, and Sword Fish.

Taking Two Large Whales in a Gale of Wind—Harpooner fastening, while the boat is high out of the water on the Whale's back; Wonderful escape.

Whale Breaching his whole length in the air; Harpooner fastening, by pitchpoling his irons into him before he strikes the water.

Ship moored to two Whales in a furious gale; Whales saved.

Boat Thrown 15 Feet into the Air—Men, lines, tubs, kegs, lances, harpoons, &c., flying in every direction.

THE LAST WHALE—Good luck; Ship full; Flags flying; Ships running down; Letters for Home.

SOCIETY ISLANDS—Otaheita; Emeo; Matavia Bay; H. B. M. sloop-of-war Acteon; U. S. sloop-of-war Vincennes; Whale ships, boats, canoes, &c.

GRAND FETE—Reception of her Tahitian Majesty, Pomare on board the British sloop-of-war; Sloop's barge conveying the Queen on board. On rounding the stern of the Vincennes she is saluted from that vessel.

HOMEWARD BOUND.

Tickets 25 Cents. Children 15 Cents.

☞ Liberal arrangements made with Schools for the Afternoon Exhibitions. ☜

Evening Performance, doors open at 6 3-4 o'clock.................To commence at 7 1-2 o'clock

Afternoons, doors open at 2 o'clock. To commence at 3 o'clock.

J. H. & F. F. Farwell, Steam Job Printers, 112 Washington Street, Boston

Programme for Williams 1860 production at the Melodeon Hall in Boston. Photo courtesy Peabody Museum of Salem.

of particular interest in the announcements and reviews are the scattered references to the painting of Williams' panorama. One such announcement attributes his panorama to "the pencil of Culvert; under the direction of experienced ship masters,"[27] while a subsequent notice informed readers that the actual painting had taken place in New York City and that the panorama had been first exhibited in Brooklyn.[28] Though the disclosures seem consistent with references already cited in Odell, they do not explain how the panorama became identified from the first with Williams or indeed just who Captain E. C. Williams was.[29]

All that can be said with certainty is that he was the panorama's delineator and perhaps rather uncertain in the job at that. On opening night at Liberty Hall on 1 October 1858, for instance, one reviewer claimed that he entered into the spirit of the scenes, yet appeared "a little embarrassed in the presence of so many whalemen, more recently from the exciting scenes than himself."[30]This same individual also noted that on the following afternoon and evening (October 2) Mr. F. Hine of Rochester [New York], an old whaleman, would take command of the ship," and from what we hear of his ability as a delineator, we anticipate a rich treat."[31]

In a somewhat different account of opening night, Captain Williams is described as not very well, and "after starting the ship on her cruise, called upon Lieut. Porter of the U.S.N. to take command, who, though not perfectly familiar with the service, succeeded quite satisfactorily in explaining the process of capturing and cutting up the leviathan of the deep."[32] The reviewer closed with the promise that Captain Williams would return the following night (October 2) to "relate in his own graphic and soul-stirring sailor's language, scenes and incidents in which he participated." To add to this confusion this same paper in a retrospective article described Williams as a tower of strength on opening night:

> *The Captain now commenced, in earnest, his delineations of the voyage, and at times when he entered upon the spirited scenes of capturing the leviathan of the deep, and depicted with graphic exactness the difficulties, dangers, incidents, and accidents the whaleman meets on the Great Ocean, he appeared almost to have believed himself for the nonce among the whalers themselves, at one time harpoon, and then lance in hand, ready to deal the deadly blow.*[33]

Disagree as the press does about the identity of the delineator at a particular performance, they are one in recording the enthusiasm of New Bedford audiences. Despite inclement weather on opening night, over 600 persons — "more than have been in the hall on a similar occasion since the lecture season" — were present and seemingly "gratified" by what they had seen.[34] Saturday afternoon and evening audiences again numbered between 600 and 700, and there was an unusually heavy turn out of ladies for the Saturday evening performance.[35]

Though Mr. Hine of Rochester, the sometime delineator, had but a few times explained the paintings, he seemed perfectly at home and speaking from actual observation, occasionally told a short yarn with as much gusto "as though he was in the forecastle of the ship."[36] The correctness and naturalness of the painting, especially the whaling scenes, brought favorable comment, and evoked a kind of running commentary that could be heard within the hall as the scenes passed before the eye: "There goes flukes!" "There she blows!" "Stern all!" So expressive were many of these remarks that "once or twice" the delineator stopped, deeming his verbal descriptions "unnecessary." But these delineations were an important contributor to the panorama's success: "The manifestations of applause, both of the delineations and of the paintings, were frequent and generally in the right place."

Following these well attended and well received showings in Fall River and New Bedford, the panorama perhaps toured other Massachusetts towns as witness a handbill in the collection of the Whaling Museum advertising on October 25-26 showings at an unknown Central Hall:

ALL HANDS WEIGH ANCHOR, AHOY!
GRAND SOUTH SEA
WHALING VOYAGE
ILLUSTRATED ON 8000 FEET OF CANVAS!
The Splendid A 1 Coppered and Copper-fastened Whale Ship
ELIZABETH STARBUCK
WILLIAMS, COMMANDER
WILL SAIL AFTERNOON & EVEN'G,
MONDAY and TUESDAY
October 25th and 26th, at 3 and 7 1-2 P.M.
From her mooring in
CENTRAL HALL

Evidently the panorama took as its focus the voyage of a particular whaleship. In this case not a ficticious creation but a vessel that did in fact exist. The *Elizabeth Starbuck* was built at Mattapoisett in 1834 and sailed out of Nantucket on her maiden voyage in that same year to return in 1837 laden with 2708 barrels of sperm oil. Subsequently, she made voyages to the whaling grounds in the Pacific Ocean in 1837-1841, 1841-1845, and 1845-1850.[37] Then in 1850 on her final voyage she was withdrawn from whaling at Hobart, Tasmania. From that port she sailed with 98 passengers for Monterey, California, where she was condemned as unseaworthy. Williams may have been a member of her crew on the 1834-1837 voyage as details included in a surviving program suggest his familiarity with the presence of foreign ships in Pacific waters in 1837;[38] however, he was never that whaleship's captain on any of her four voyages, and his command of the *Elizabeth Starbuck* and was confined to the painted vessel.[39]

The second section of the handbill gives further particulars:

Passage 15 cents. *Children 10 cents.*
INCLUDING CABIN FARE OF THE CHOICEST KIND
Tickets to be obtained at the Captain's Office on board, on the

> *day of sailing. Passengers will please on coming on board, present their tickets to the officer of the deck and he will order the stewards to conduct them to their respective berths. The Captain has made the comfort of Ladies his particular study, reserving for them portions of the ship where the motion will be least annoying, and views unobstructed.*

The final segment is perhaps of greatest interest as it details the "program of the Voyage," which was divided into three sections. Part one, of the first section, perhaps not part of the panorama proper, focused attention on a chart to which the delineator pointed as he "laid down the courses and distances sailed and the places touched at by whale ships generally; the feeding-grounds of the Sperm whale and the wonderful polar and ocean current." Commencing with part two of section one, the panorama opened with a view of Nantucket harbor; then, following the sailing out of the harbor, the viewer saw scenes reminiscent of what Russell had given his audiences. Part three, the final segment of the first section, was devoted to Crossing the line. The second section opened with the view of a ship on fire and closed with an exhibition of the various implements used in the capture of the Leviathan.

The introduction of these implements must have served as a natural bridge to the opening of the third section, devoted almost exclusively to the iconography of whaling, beginning with the whaleship at the cruising grounds with men at the masthead and culminating in the intense physical activity of cutting in. Full of oil, at length the whaler headed for the Society Islands and on anchoring found herself near such other vessels as *H.B.M. Acteon* and the U.S. sloop-of-war *Vincennes*. A Grand Fete was held aboard the *Acteon*, whose highpoint was the reception of her Tahitian Majesty Pomare on board the British vessel. In the wake of these festivities the *Elizabeth Starbuck* headed for home and Williams brought his delineation to a close. No doubt his audience dispersed feeling, as the final segment of the handbill promised, that they had themselves been in pursuit of the Leviathan.

Following this unidentified showing, the panorama dropped from sight to reappear a little more than a year later in Erie, Pennsylvania. There, various scenes were "well explained by Capt. Williams, who accompanied the voyage, and who has personal knowledge of all therein set forth."[40] Then on to Cleveland, Ohio, where promotional materials reiterated the fact that the panorama was "from the pencil of Culvert, under the direction of experienced ship masters."[41] One announcement described the panorama as being 8000 feet in length, but in the absence of supporting evidence "8000 feet" is very probably a publicist's exaggeration — witness Russell's advertised "three miles."[42] Williams' Cleveland delineation was also applauded in terms reminiscent of earlier commentary: not pretending "to any of the rhetorical flourishes of a self-styled professor," he narrated the scene in "plain commonsense language."[43]

Dropping from sight for the remainder of the winter, the panorama surfaced in New London, Connecticut, at Lawrence Hall early in April 1860,[44] and the reportorial commentary, commencing on April 4, reflected the good press Williams seems generally to have enjoyed. Reference is made to a large and appreciative audience on opening night and apparently the panorama fully sustained for New London audiences the recommendations given it by New Bedford, Nantucket and the journals of other whaling ports. For New Londoners as a work of art it defied criticism, "being a series of thrilling pictures truthfully illustrating the life and experiences of the American Whaleman."[45] Captain Williams was on hand as host and rarely failed "to convulse his audience with laughter and interest them with his graphic descriptions of scenes through which he has passed and witnessed."

Following an afternoon showing for young people with specially reduced rate — children 6 cents, parents 10 cents — "this truly interesting and instructive exhibition" moved on to showings like that at Waterbury, Connecticut, for which a flyer survives in the collection of The Kendall Whaling Museum. The handbill, advertising Williams' "Grand South Sea Whaling Voyage" at Hotchkiss Hall on 17 August 1860 resembles the Central Hall bill save that admissions are up — passage tickets 25 cents, children under 12 years of age 10 cents. For an upcoming Saturday afternoon performance: tickets 15 cents, children 10 cents. The program that is included as part of the flyer is identical to that printed on the earlier bill.

Williams was out to attract the widest possible audience *via* afternoon and evening performances at admissions geared to what the traffic would bear. As evidenced, too, by the account of the initial children's showing at Fall River, he was apt to gear his presentation to the audience he faced in a particular performance, and it seems evident that modifications in his materials occurred from time to time. One of the most interesting of these took place at the Hotchkiss Hall showing though it is not included in the program already referred to. The Waterbury press described it as the climax of the performance: "From the crosstrees the cry comes in true sailor style, 'There she blows!' And now all is confusion on deck. The Captain shouting to his imaginary men strips off his coat at this juncture, springs into his whaling boat [standing in front of the platform], catches up the steering oar, and apparently forgetting his audience and imagining himself on the ocean once more . . . goes through all the operations . . . which would be necessary at such a time. . . . "[46] Though it is not clear from the text of the review, this addition seems to have been interpolated into the program without announcement.

It was an established feature, however, by the time of the Springfield, Massachusetts' showing in October and November 1860.[47] To this community Williams brought "private testimonials" both as to the high character of the panorama and to himself, and his opening performance was crowned with success. Crowded houses nightly followed, drawn by what one reporter described as "a faithful transcript of the life, business, duties and excitements accompanying a whaling voyage."[48] Williams is revealed as an "experienced exhibitor" who was successful in presenting "a large mass of useful knowledge without being tedious." Assisting him on October 20 at afternoon and evening performances for the benefit of school children and others

The whaleman's sleigh ride. Plates from *Life in the South Seas* by Capt. E. C. Williams (New York: Polhemus and DeVries, 1860). Courtesy of Charles F. Batchelder.

was a Captain Henry A. Phelon of West Springfield, who it was promised would take charge of the boat and officiate as harpooner.[49]

Phelon, the son of Henry Phelon Jr., one of Nantucket's whaling captains, had himself made at least one whaling voyage aboard his father's ship, the *Plough Boy*. In 1860 he had only recently returned from a decade in California where he had been successively a gold hunter and master of a coastal trader. Thus, he was presumably entitled to the title of "captain" by which the press addressed him.[50] Whether or not he assisted Williams in the days that followed is not clear, but the panorama's Springfield press continued to be unusually good. And on what was announced as the final evening, a great crowd was on hand to present Captain Williams with a complimentary resolution urging him to continue his exhibiton: "There is no doubt that more valuable and correct information is obtained of the wonders, labor and perils of whalemen by one evening's presence at your exhibition, than from all the books on the subject."[51]

It is no wonder that after an "interruption" Williams reappeared on 1 November at the Music Hall, presumably assisted by Phelon, who had purchased one half of the exhibition for 2000 dollars.[52] The latter must have had his work cut out for him as Williams rounded out his stay with evening performances through November 3 and advertised a free afternoon showing for Springfield's sunday school children on 1 November. The encomiums of Springfield ringing in his ears, Williams headed for Boston where his "soul-stirring" exhibition opened at the Melodeon on 9 November 1860 without mention of Captain Phelon in any of the publicity materials.[53] What makes this showing of particular interest is the existence of a handbill and a pamphlet, which may have served as a souvenir program of sorts for showings in Boston and elsewhere.

The handbill, advertising Williams' fifth week at the Melodeon, describes the panorama as a "Brilliant Success" and notes performances every evening during the week as well as Wednesday and Saturday afternoons.[54] The text calls on viewers not to confound "A South Sea Whaling Voyage" with "other Exhibitions" — which may be an oblique reference to Russell's panorama. Williams is referred to as "Captain" and he is said to have followed the sea "as Cabin Boy, Mate, and Captain, through all the various grades for nearly Thirty Years." The veracity of these bibliographical references is unknown, though as it has been mentioned, it is unlikely that Williams had been the captain of a whaler.[55] Nevertheless, he was probbly qualified to delineate what the handbill calls his description of "Life on the Ocean Wave."

The program of the "voyage," included on the handbill, is divided into two sections rather than the three of the Central Hall flyer. The first section's three parts cover the scenes previously included in sections one and two, beginning with the chart and ending with the exhibition of implements. The second section begins with "the Thrilling Boat Scene" (now formalized in the program) and includes all of what the Central Hall showing had included in the third section of that handbill. Evidently these revisions were very much to the taste of Boston audiences as was the music promised in connection with the scenery by Miss Murdock and Prof. Fernald. Prices were up, too. The Central Hall bill had listed passage at 15 cents for adults and 10 cents for children. Bostonians paid 25 cents and 15 cents respectively from 9 November 1860 to 12 January 1861.

Many who were intrigued by Williams' presentation no doubt paid out money for a pamphlet titled *Life in the South Seas. History of the Whale Fisheries. Habits of the Whale. Perils of the Chase and Method of Capture* by Captain E. C. Williams, who is listed on the title page as "Delineator of Williams' Panorama of a South Sea Whaling Voyage."[56] An appendage to the overlong title includes the following: "Startling Incidents — Graphic Delinations — Thrilling Scenes in the life of the American Whaleman, Compiled from Various Writers and The Author's Personal Experiences of the Scenes Described." Unfortunately there is nothing of Williams' personal experience in the thirty-odd pages of the pamphlet available to Boston purchasers. It is all too obviously a hasty compilation of materials grabbed at random from then available literature on whaling. Included are such familiar names as Herman Melville, Miriam Coffin and J. Ross Browne.[57] One would have hoped that Williams' thirty years at sea would have resulted in a contribution from his own experience but the searcher looks in vain. Evidently the captain was saving what he had to offer for his panoramic delineations.

Following a complimentary benefit for Williams the panorama headed for Salem where it opened at Mechanic Hall on January 14.[58] A notice in the press, calling attention to "the famous exhibition," suggested that those interested look at the picture in the store window of D. B. Brooks and Brother.[59] Unfortunately there is no indication as to its nature. The *Salem Gazette* included a longish review that lauded Williams' interesting and instructive exhibition and called on residents not only of Salem but of neighboring towns to get up a sleighing party or two and attend the panoramic exhibition.[60] Williams, described as a whaler, is said to make no pretensions as either an orator or a delineator, "and evidently has an idea that he has a very homely and uncouth way of doing things in this line, — we hesitate not to say that he is really the best delineator we ever heard describe a panorama of this kind."

The reviewer goes on to single out an inclusion by Williams in the program that has not been noted earlier and perhaps was only a recent addition, this his telling of the story of a little boy who died on board a whaling ship, "and the description of his ocean burial, was really a pathetic and affecting narration, which a long training in the arts of oratory could not have excelled." The *Gazette's* account is especially helpful in that it makes clear that the chart alluded to as early as the Fall River exhibition was not an integral part of the panorama but rather "a simple outline map" of North and South America used to convey an idea of the course pursued to the whaling ground, indicated by dark patches." Once it had served its purpose, it was withdrawn and the panorama began to move.

Mention is made by the paper's reviewer of the exotic geography to be seen and he gives special attention to the Captain's exhibition of the implements of whaling. Then he tells his readers that Williams manned a full-sized whale boat with "a regular crew," who assisted him in acting out the entire whaling experience: "We cannot attempt to describe this performance, which could scarcely be more spirited if aided by a live whale, and the faithfullness of which is full attested to by those present who have been on whaling voyages." His account brings the moment to life: "The long pull, the mishaps of the green boys, the chagrin of the harpooner who missed fire, the blowing up of the Boat Header in consequence, the falling asleep while heading for the ship at night after a hard day's pull."

Phelon had been associated with the boat scene in the Springfield performance but his name had not been connected with it or with co-ownership of the panorama in the Boston or Salem papers. However, he is listed in connection with the former in the showing in Portland, Maine, which ran at Lancaster Hall from 5 March 1861, to 21 March.[61] Phelon may or may not have been in charge of it but he is listed as rendering a boat song. There was also a chorus by the crew, perhaps another of Williams' refinements.[62] The Portland press favored Williams throughout his engagement, claiming that his panorama had something more to it than "Dabs of gaudy paint spread upon canvas, for mere show."[63] In the eyes of one correspondent this panorama was "much superior" to the general run, and as an entertainment "very amusing."[64] The boat scene received his commendation and in now familiar language he maintained that Williams' panorama gave "a more vivid idea of the perils, excitements, and disappointments of a whaleman's life than can be obtained in any other way."

One wonders how Williams managed to get all his paraphenalia about the country. The great rolls of canvas must have presented their problems, not to mention that full-sized whaleboat. If its crew travelled with the show, the panorama's entourage must have been impressive. Or were they hired as was many a supernumerary in the theatre of the day — that is off the street? Perhaps an advance agent sought out former whalemen in the cities to be visited and engaged them for the run of the show. Whatever the case, Williams probably preferred to remain profitably in one spot as long as possible. And among his longest known runs was that at Hope Chapel in New York City, to which the captain came with his "Grand Nautical Exhibition" early in October 1861. He remained into April of the next year.[65]

His patrons had the opportunity during Williams' tenure at Hope Chapel to purchase yet another edition of the pamphlet that had been available to Bostonians. This 68 page booklet, including essentially the same text as the earlier edition, was distinguished by ten colored lithographs (approximately 3 by 4¾ inches) on stiff white paper.[66] Waves, whales and boats are all in a "purple red" while clouds are shown in a light blue; and though the foreground waves are in violent agitation, the backgrounds are most "pacific."[67] The scenes depicted are variously designated "Outward Bound," "Arrival upon the Whaling Ground," "The Whaleman's Sleigh Right," "Boat Destroyed by the Jaw," "Boat Destroyed by the Whales Flukes," "The Harpoon," "The Lance," "The Death Flurry," "Cutting In," and "Homeward Bound." These titles correspond roughly to the details listed on the programs of the three handbills previously referred to and it is tempting to identify them with Williams' panorama. Unfortunately there is no real justification for doing so. Very possibly Williams borrowed them as he had the excerpts from his various authorities, though he did not indicate his source.[68]

The principal addition to the text of this pamphlet consisted of the inclusion of a longish review from the *New York Daily Tribune* which praised Williams "Muscular lecture" in extravagant language.[69] The author depicted "whale-catching" as "the wildest dream of arch-courage" and for him nothing was more romantically inspiring or superbly bold "than to advance in the tiny boat with the slender lance upon the monster of monsters, to strike, to kill, to capture it, and to render its remains subservient to the grandest purposes of civilization — in defying the black night and shedding to luster of day over the still, small hours." The *Tribune's* readers are told that if they doubt the "ultra peril" of whaling, they should go hear and see Williams in the basement of Hope Chapel, "now consecrated to the world of the flesh — the devil being left out, for the present at least."

Williams is characterized in a prose style that is worth quoting in its entirety:

> *The gallant Captain is the concentrated essence of the best specimen of the Jack-Tar. Except for a limited period required for his birth, first detention, and the acquisiton of Newenglish, the Captain has spent his life on the far waters, harpooning their oleaginous tribes. He looks, speaks, and walks the sea. He is the salt of the earth. If the Captain had not been of Nantucket, where whales are preferred to the regular drama, he would probably have been stage-struck instead of whale-struck, for he has qualities for an actor. Not all the hardening of rough winds and exposures has stricken from his epidermis the mobility due the expression of the histrionic man. He acts out the whaler. He has the machinery, less the whale and less the water, to do so.*

Of course, what the reviewer refers to when he writes of acting out the whaler is the by now familiar boat scene — apparently less Phelon. His description amplifies that already quoted from the Salem papers and there appear several additional touches that very probably pleased. To quote again:

> *On the stage there is a whale-boat, provided with harpoons, ropes, oars, sailors. The whole tragedy and comedy of whale-catching, not marred by blood or coarseness, are represented by the captain and his crew. They row; they throw out the line; they strain at the oar; the comic sailor lad falls overboard; they harpoon one watery brute, and miss another; they fall asleep with over-exertion; the captain precedes and postcedes this practical display of the art by reciting, dramatically, technical and romantic matter connected with it. . . .*

Though the text is ambiguous, it is quite possible that moving segments of the panorama provided a scenic backdrop to this moment in the program;

and at more than one point, unseen musicians "discourse sweet and applicable music and verse." The grand finale, as described by the article, was one most appropriate to the day and reveals something of Williams' interpolated bits of showmanship. At that point when the whaler is shown at anchor in the Society Islands "the inevitable flag is let fall before the audience, and the inevitable Star-Spangled Banner stirs the nerves of the audience." Commenting on Williams' inspirational touch, the *Tribune's* reviewer proclaimed he had witnessed "great vital work: that of the country nourishing her sons in the strength, and courage, and address, without which Liberty and Unity cannot thrive and be enduring."

The captain, perhaps caught up in the *Tribune's* rhetoric himself, may have answered his nation's call for volunteers, for the panorama dropped from sight for more than a year. The next known showing of his whaling voyage was at Troy, New York's Rand Hall in the fall of 1863.[70] An account book kept by the Rand family shows Williams at their hall from 23 November through 2 December 1863, and again from 24 March through 28 March 1866.[71] Unfortunately this record is little more than a bald compilation of dates and attractions. For instance, Williams was preceded in November 1863 by such attractions as a Lecture on Hair, Father Kemp Old Folks and the Morris Minstrels and followed in December by Prof. A. O'Leary, Sullivan's Band Concert and Stanley Conant's Panorama — subject matter unspecified. When he returned in March 1866 his panorama was but one of many attractions that crowded the month. These included the Peak Family, a glass blowing act, and Tony Pastor and Sam Sharply.

Yet another New York community which welcomed Williams at least twice was Syracuse. Here he played early in January 1864, and subsequently in March 1866, just prior to his second visit to Troy, also with the "real Whale-Boat and crew."[72] On the occasion of this second visit one of the Syracuse papers included a complimentary notice which is the most fullsome praise of the panorama's promoter yet; it is reproduced in full:

> *The American stage, or any other stage, never yet was trod by a "star" having in a greater degree the power to move the general heart, than does our "jolly tar" in his recitals of whaling adventures on the stormy deep. The rollicking freedom with which he describes the fierce, reckless daring of the Yankee "salt" in his encounters with the lord of the ocean, makes the pulse of the hearer to throb in strongest sympathy, exciting the fancy to almost actual participation in the heroism of whale hunting. All qualities of heart and brain necessary to arouse and carry the listener captive, are his. There is no cessation, no abatement of interest during the entire evening; and not until the curtain falls, and the captain's earnest voice sinks to the key of announcement of the next evening's entertainment, is the audience made aware of the passage of time.*[73]

A most interesting ad calling on the citizens of Syracuse to turn out for the four-day showing, makes mention of Williams having completed all the

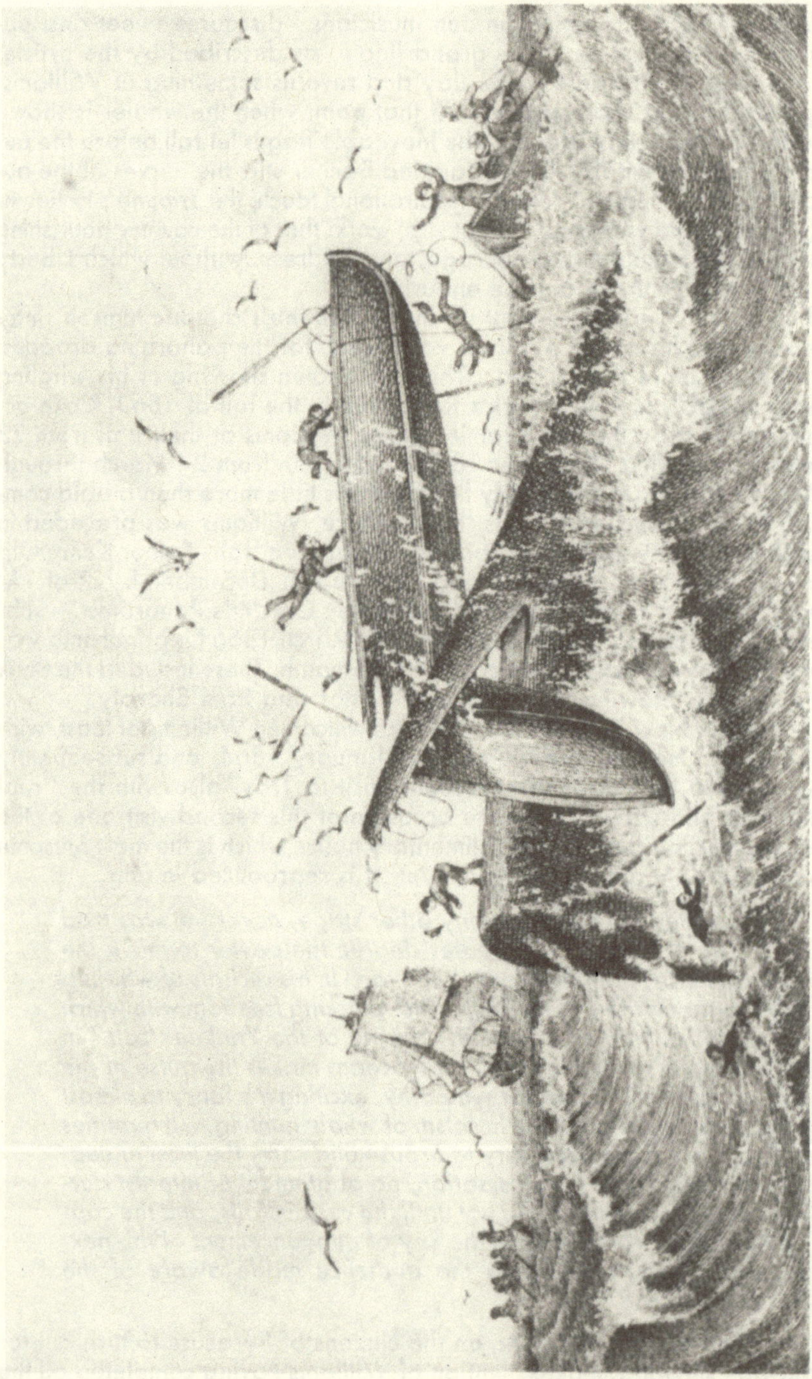

Boat destroyed by the jaws. Plates from *Life in the South Seas* by Capt. E. C. Williams (New York: Polhemus and DeVries, 1860). Courtesy of Charles F. Batchelder.

arrangements for a tour of England.[74] Readers were told he was to sail from New York in the steamship *Fulton* on June 6. Prior to these dates the copy announces the panorama was to be seen in Troy commencing 24 March and in Albany for four weeks beginning 29 March and closing 26 April. Perhaps predictably the Troy papers played up "the last opportunity" theme, calling on its readers to view the "Greatest Exhibition of the Age" prior to its English engagement.[75] And in an opening day notice one paper made known the fact that since the whaling voyage was last in Troy, the panorama had been improved and several new features added. Unfortunately these changes are not documented.

The Albany showing, presumably the final appearance before the European venture, opened 29 March as announced. But an advertisement placing it at Association Hall indicated that the panorama was to remain only for one week rather than the month promised in the Syracuse and Troy papers.[77] Of some interest in the text of this ad is the reference to scenes in the life of a Nantucket Whaleman being illustrated by "TABLEAU VIVANTS or Living pictures." Perhaps these were among the improvements noted in Troy, but there is no indication as to their nature — just possibly the reference is to the boat scene. The ad in question places emphasis upon the "magnificent" panoramic views being drawn from the captain's "own personal adventures," a point certainly made earlier but not quite so emphatically.

Just possibly in this emphasis there is an explanation of the *Elizabeth Starbuck*, becoming unexpectedly the goodship *Martha*, a transformation noted in the Syracuse press. Surviving records indicate that there was only one *Elizabeth Starbuck* and while Williams may have served on her as a cabin boy or seaman, he was certainly not her captain at any time. On the other hand, there were some ten whaleships' named *Martha* in service between 1787 and 1874 and at least one of these vessels was active in the trade in 1866.[78] In numbers there was safety.

At this point, given the notices of a foray amid English audiences, we should look for Williams' sailing from the port of New York. However, it is very possible that he did not do so. For, when heard from again, he is at Corinthian Hall in Rochester, New York.[79] To sail from New York City in June, tour England and return in time to start a new American tour and be in upper New York state by November is possible but rather improbable. Equally puzzling is that following the Rochester showing Williams' panorama drops from sight and no further exhibitions are known — at least to this author — which is not to say, of course, that they did not take place.[80] But as in the case of Russell's panorama as many nagging questions are left unanswered as resolved. Equally frustrating is that barring some lucky windfall of fresh material the story of America's whaling panoramas is likely to remain tantalizingly incomplete.

Appearing on the scene during whaling's golden age, the panoramas in question played to audiences living where whaling was a near or present reality and to those in the hinterlands for whom it had few if any immediate associations. Yet both audiences found pleasure in the viewing experience.

Apollo Building in Cincinnati, Ohio, where Russell's panorama was exhibited in late December 1849 and early January 1850. Photo dated 1851. Courtesy the Cincinnati Historical Society.

Those familiar with whaling testified repeatedly — if the press is to be believed — to the veracity of the panoramas and many former whalemen must have relived the drama of their youth as the moving canvas passed before them. For literally thousands of others far removed from the geographic area of the whaling industry but citizens of a mid-century America there was, as many an advertisement promised, not only the vicarious excitement to be enjoyed in the pictorial pursuit of the mighty leviathan of the ocean but the romantic lure of picturesque and exotic scenery.

Panoramas existed as countless promotional and review materials tell us to instruct and entertain. No doubt both the efforts of Russell and Williams were eminently satisfactory in the former category but this writer has the feeling that as quasi-theatrical entertainment Williams' presentation had the edge with audiences of the day. The good Captain seems the more astute showman and promoter, altering and modifying his materials to find that blend of adventure, spectacle and sentiment needed to win the favor of his audience. No matter, the point to remember is that both panoramas achieved what no print or series of prints or erudite history of whaling was able to do — namely encompass for American audiences the complexities of an industry, even as they gave flesh and color to a way of life and to a breed of men personifying an ideal manhood. With conscious intent the panoramas of American whaling capitalized on the evocation of place as they did upon the magic formula evoked by the hoarse shout from the masthead, "Thar she blows! — Thar she breaches!"

NOTES

[1]Though there is no comprehensive study of the genre available, the opening chapter of John Francis McDermott's *The Lost Panoramas of the Mississippi* (Chicago, 1958) is helpful. Among a scattering of articles in a wide range of journals Charlotte Willard's "Panoramas, the First Movies," *Art in America* (no. 4, 1959), pp. 65-69, is representative. Art historians who touch on panoramic fare include Wolfgang Born, *American Landscape Painting* (New Haven, 1948); Oliver Larkin, *Art and Life in America* (New York, 1949), Virgil Barker, *American Painting* (New York, 1950); and James T. Flexner, *That Wilder Image* (New York, 1962).

[2]Details of the New Bedford showing are found in the archives of The Whaling Museum, whose records indicate the panorama returned the following summer and was in New Bedford at least on 24 July 1849.

[3]In the collection of The Whaling Museum. According to Nathaniel Dearborn's *Reminiscences of Boston and Guide Through the City and Environs,* Amory Hall, built in 1835, consisted of three stories, having three stores on the lower floor and two large halls above for public meetings; one hall could accommodate 600 persons and the other 300. Its original address was 323 Washington Street, changed in 1875 after the fire to 503.

[4]Issue for 11 January 1849.

[5]Issue for 23 January 1849.

[6]Issue for 30 January 1849.

[7]Handbill referred to above is dated in ink April 2d, 1849.

[8]From the *Buffalo Morning Express,* 28 November 1859. The panorama was shown in Buffalo between 26 November and 3 December. Local papers ran the identical ad day after day without alteration, which must have confused those readers who came upon it the final day it appeared. The Clinton Hall site, the southeast corner of Washington and Clinton Streets, is now occupied by the Lafayette Hotel.

[9]Samuel P. Orth's *A History of Cleveland, Ohio* described Empire Hall as one of the city's most important halls seating some 600. It stood at the corner of Superior and Bank streets, now West Superior and West 6th Streets.

[10]*Daily True Democrat*, 14 December 1849.

[11]*Evening Herald*, 13 December 1849.

[12]The panorama opened in Cincinnati about 24 December 1849 and continued until 9 January 1850 and probably for a short time thereafter.

[13]*Gazette*, 24, 28, 29, 31 December 1849.

[14]*Ibid.*, 1 January 1850.

[15]*Ibid.*, 9 January 1850.

[16]*Daily Gazette*, 23 February 1850. Just when the panorama opened in Pittsburgh is not clear but its final night was apparently the 23rd. Curiously the ads do not indicate the hall in which Russell's canvas was exhibited.

[17]*Daily Journal*, 29 March 1850.

[18]*Ibid.*

[19]*Ibid.*, 30 March 1850.

[20]Gabriel Collins'; *Louisville and New Albany Directory* (1848) locates Apollo Rooms at Third Street between Main and Market. It was one of 13 public halls listed in White's *Louisville Directory* (1855-56).

[21]Issue for 19 April 1850.

[22]Issue for 20 February 1851.

[23]Issue for 10 September 1851.

[24]See especially vols. V-VII.

[25]Odell VII, p. 104-107.

[26]*Fall River Beacon*, 25 September 1858; reprinted in *The New Bedford Daily Mercury*, 30 September 1858.

[27]*Daily Mercury*, 30 September 1858. Spelling *Culvert* every conceivable way, it is impossible to uncover his identity in sources like Groce's *The New York Historical Society's Dictionary of Artists in America*. M. V. Brewington of The Kendall Whaling Museum, an acknowledged authority on the visual history of whaling, reports no more success in sources available to him.

[28]*Ibid.*, 4 October 1858.

[29]A possible clue to Williams' identity is found in a testimonial letter from a James S. Tryon, cashier of the Merchants and Manufacturers' Bank, Hartford, Conn. This letter dated 12 May 1860 reprinted in *The Waterbury American*, 17 August 1860, mentions the banker's acquaintance with Williams from 1848 to 1857. During these years Tryon was a resident of Rochester, New York, leaving that city for Hartford in 1857. A search of Rochester's city directories reveals an Edward C. Williams beginning in 1844. His occupation is given as sailmaker. Subsequent directories list him variously as sailmaker and ship furnisher (1849-50), sail and tent maker (1857). He disappears from the directories after 1857. Presumably he removed to the New York City area to direct Culvert in the painting of the panorama. When his panorama appeared in Rochester in November 1866, *The Union And Advertiser* referred to him as "our old townsman," which seems to bear on Edward C. Williams and Captain E. C. Williams being one and the same individual.

[30]*Daily Evening Standard*, 2 October 1858.

[31]The Rochester directories list a vareity of F. Hines from 1851-1859, though the occupations listed provide no real clue as to which Hine might have been a sometime whaleman.

[32]*Daily Mercury*, 2 October 1858.

[33]*Ibid.*, 4 October 1858.

[34]*Daily Evening Standard*, 2 October 1858.

[35]*Daily Mercury*, 4 October 1858.

[36]*Ibid.*

[37]Alexander Starbuck, *History of American Whale Fisher* (New York, 1964), pp. 308, 376, 426.

[38]Charles F. Batchelder of Boston, Mass., points out that the Boston program describes a scene showing *H.B.M. Acteon* and *U.S.S. Vincennes* in Tahiti when presumably Williams was there. Both vessels were in the Pacific in 1837; *Acteon* was back in England early in 1838.

Williams, on being paid off, may have made his way to Rochester, New York, and set himself up as a sailmaker.

[39]Starbuck lists the following captains: Obed Cathcart (1834-37) Henry Bigelow (1841-45), Elijah Parker (1845-1850).

[40]*Weekly Gazette*, 1 December 1859.

[41]Announcements in the Cleveland press indicate Williams opened 20 December 1859, at Melodeon Hall, formerly Watson Hall, on the 2nd floor of a structure located on Superior Street between Seneca and Bank Streets. It seated a thousand persons comfortably. Probably the panorama remained into early January. The last recorded reference to it in the Cleveland press appeared on 30 December.

[42]*Cleveland Leader*, 22 December 1859.

[43]*Ibid.*, 26 December 1859.

[44]Lawrence Hall, completed in 1856, was the principal hall in New London for lectures and exhibitions. Caulkin's *History of New London* claims it was beautiful in decoration, proportion and interior accommodations. It could seat 1200 people.

[45]*Weekly Chronicle*, 4 April 1860.

[46]*The Waterbury American*, 17 August 1860. The boat scene was added perhaps as early as the New Haven, Conn., showing, which opened at Brewster's Hall on 22 June and continued until 7 July at which time Williams moved to Fair Haven (a suburb of New Haven) and remained until 17 July. Then apparently he returned to New Haven's National Hall, remaining until 28 July. *The Daily Palladium* (23 July 1860) includes a letter from him to the public which reads in part: "Having obtained a whale-boat, which I intend arranging in front of the stage and fitting up with all the paraphernalia . . . & by my taking all the various positions of the whalemen in active pursuit and capture, I flatter myself that I shall be enabled to give a more startling effect to the scenes as they pass." Whether the boat scene was included in the Bridgeport, Conn., showing which followed that in New Haven, is not clear from the 4 August ad in *The Bridgeport Daily Standard*.

[47]Williams appeared at the Music Hall. Erected shortly after the financial depression of 1857, it was destroyed by fire. The lower floors were occupied by stores while the second floor was devoted entirely to concerts and lectures.

[48]*Daily Republican*, 18 October 1860.

[49]*Ibid.*, 20 October 1860.

[50]Details of Phelon's life and career are drawn from his obituary printed in the *Springfield Daily Republican*, 2 April, 1902.

[51]*Daily Republican*, 25 October 1860.

[52]*Ibid.*, 29 October 1860. He was not Williams' first partner. This distinction may have gone to a man named Fowler. At the close of the 4 week Hartford, Conn., showing which had commenced on 19 April 1860, the local press speculated that Fowler would probably "take the whales to Middletown next week."

[53]Williams remained until 12 January. An ad appeared in the *Boston Transcript* beginning 13 November and continued through 12 January. In addition, under the "Boston: about home affairs," there was almost daily a notice of an informative rather than critical nature pertaining to the panorama. Ads for the opening appeared also in the *Boston Post* and *The Boston Daily Evening Traveller*.

[54]In the collection of Francis B. Lothrop, an honorary trustee of the Peabody Museum, Salem, Mass.

[55]See note 29. If E. C. Williams was, indeed, Edward C. Williams, a sometime resident of Rochester, N.Y., these biographical notes seem suspect. Perhaps for a brief time he could have been the captain of an Erie Canal boat — a far cry from commanding a Yankee whaler.

[56]Published both in Boston and New York in 1860, The New York edition is over the imprint: Polhemus and Devries, Printers; The Boston edition: J. H. and F. F. Farwell, printers, 112 Washington St.

[57]The pamphlet is divided into sections with such headings as "The Whale," "Whaling Life," "The Line," "Indians Whaling" — to name only the first four. Following some, though not all, of the sections is an acknowledgement. The "Line," for instance, is credited "Herman Melville." Only two sections are credited to a specific work: one to *Moby Dick*, the other to J. Ross Browne's *Etchings of a Whaling Cruise*.

[58]Mechanic Hall, according to Osgood and Batchelder's *Sketch of Salem,* stood on the corner of Essex and Crombie Streets. It was the largest and finest hall in that city.

[59]*Salem Register*, 14 January 1861.

[60]*Salem Gazette*, 18 January 1861.

[61]Lancaster Hall is first listed in *The Portland City Directory* for 1856-1857 as standing on the corner of Center and Congress Streets. It accommodated 800 persons.

[62]*The Eastern Argus*, 18 March 1861.

[63]*Ibid.*, 8 March 1861.

[64]*The Portland Transcript*, 16 March 1861.

[65]Odell, VII, p. 444.

[66]Published in New York City in 1862 by John F. Trow, Printer, 50 Green Street.

[67]Details furnished by Charles F. Batchelder are based on a copy of the pamphlet and plates in his possession.

[68]M. V. Brewington describes them in *Kendall Whaling Museum Prints* as a "series of ten postcards depicting whaling scenes."

[69]Issue for 15 November 1861.

[70]Rand Hall served Troy as a concert room, lecture hall and place for exhibitions. In 1872 it was enlarged and fitted for dramatic representations.

[71]In the collection of the Rensaelaer County History Society, Troy, New York.

[72]*Syracuse Journal*, 4 January 1864.

[73]*Ibid.*, 3 March 1866. Quoted from the *Erie Dispatch*.

[74]*Ibid.*, 17 March 1866.

[75]*Troy Daily Times*, 21 March 1866.

[76]*Ibid.*

[77]*Albany Argus*, 28 March 1866.

[78]Letter to the author from Charles F. Batchelder, dtd. 29 June 1870.

[79]*Rochester Union and Advertiser*, 26 November 1866.

[80]It is interesting to note that the last known showing occurred in Rochester, the sometime residence of Edward C. Williams. On familiar ground once more he may well have retired from the road.

The Naturalistic Bias in Criticism at the Turn of the Century vs. Lillian Mortimer

Rosemarie K. Bank

Actor-author-manager Lillian Mortimer (c. 1880-1946) began producing her own plays and presenting them on the Stair and Havlin ten-twenty-thirty circuit in 1903. She designed the costumes and scenery, served as stage manager, acted the soubrette/waif line, and did the ads for a company she managed with her husband. Her play for 1903-04, *Shadow of the Gallows*, allowed her to clear $10,000 for the season[1] and success continued until 1908 when receipts declined sharply, for example: the season of 1906-07 (*A Man's Broken Promise*) she grossed $8,000 for a week in Pittsburgh, while in 1907-08 (*Bunco in Arizona*) that gross was $7,000 for the week, and in 1908-09 (*A Girl's Best Friend*) the week produced a gross of only $2,200.[2] She gave up her company and became a headliner on the Keith vaudeville circuit, appearing in comic sketches largely of her own authorship from 1909 to about 1930, after which she retired.

At first glance, there appears to be nothing remarkable about the rise and fall of Lillian Mortimer's melodrama company. We know, for example, that with "The Great Train Robbery" in 1903, action melodramas of the sort Mortimer wrote were particularly vulnerable to losing the largely working class audience favoring them, the same audience which up to 1912 was the mainstay of films.[3] Movies could not only portray sensational scenes more graphically, they were also initially cheaper than ten-twenty-thirty (movies were still five cents in 1912), and the new houses built for films (eg., the Strand in New York in 1914) were both more comfortable and much more luxurious than the outlying, popular priced legitimate theatres that were home to Mortimer's plays.[4] Yet films were not alone the problem, as one New York reviewer makes clear by reporting that as a result of low receipts in the 1907-08 season, four popular priced theatres in the city went to vaudeville, two more became touring houses for "society" melodramas, three went over to stock companies, and only one of the ten converted to films.[5] Clearly, something was happening to the public's taste in theatre and that change is remarkable, I think, in that critics helped establish it.

According to newspaper articles, many of which she and her husband wrote, Lillian Mortimer appears to have had a divided mind about her plays. On the one side, she freely confessed in 1904 that she wrote for money, tried to appeal to audiences not of the highest social level, laughed a lot

Rosemarie K. Bank is presently a visiting professor at the University of California at Santa Barbara. Her articles have appeared in *Theatre Journal*, *Theatre Survey*, and *Theatre Studies*, etc.

off-stage at the absurd situations her characters got into, and stated there was not much art about her writing, describing her melodrama as "a cheap sort of amusement that a certain set of public always like."[6] She allowed stories that she dashed off her plays to appear unchallenged,[7] and even confessed she "would, maybe, rather be in higher branches of the profession."[8] Some reviews of this period mirror her tone, mocking *No Mother to Guide Her* and the playing of it, for example, while grudgingly granting its popularity with audiences.[9] On the other side, however, Mortimer tried to dispel the idea that she was in any way ashamed of her work, declaring that by infusing human nature into her plays she taught moral lessons.[10] By 1907, articles emphasize that sensational melodramas were hard to write, and that her plays were not really suitable for the outlying popular priced houses in which they appeared, where rough, action packed, improbable stuff was preferred.[11] Ambiguously, she seemed to disparage this audience's demand for an obvious moral,[12] yet to defend that demand,[13] declaring emphatically in 1909 that it was lurid melodramas like *Dealers in White Women* and *The Millionaire and the Policeman's Wife* that drove away her middle-class audience, largely of women and children.[14]

Periodically, Mortimer proposed to return to melodrama, predicting in 1913 that melodrama's audience was still there, as popular Broadway plays demonstrated,[15] but conceding by 1916 that when melodrama returned it would be minus the blood and thunder.[16] Critics and audiences were unaffected by her plays' high moral tone and unconvinced by her attempts to separate her work from the "gun and knife drama." The burlesques of popular priced melodramas by audiences in the 1907-08 season[17] rather attest to the validity of Mortimer's conclusion in 1909 that her brand of melodrama had "outlived itself."[18]

Like the writers of many accounts of this period, Lillian Mortimer did not totally understand what was happening at the end of the first decade of the twentieth century. Certainly, films had an impact upon popular priced melodrama, as did managers' responses to films, the Syndicate, and greater freedom in subject matter and expression on the stage, but a major cause for the decline in melodrama in 1908-09 actually began to appear in the 1890's. Not unlike Mortimer's feelings about her plays, the critical view of melodrama expressed between 1890 and 1910 is at times ambiguous, confused, contradictory, patronizing, hostile, ignorant, and biased, as accounts of this genre have been in the years since, even among scholars who are supposed to know better. To reconstruct the critical activity that created, in part, this change in public taste, we need to examine criticism in the 1890's.

Not surprisingly, the 1890's present us with yet another social change influencing theatre, this one due to a swelling population. The number of newspapers and circulation of them nationwide grew enormously from 1875 to 1900. Tice Miller, in *Bohemians and Critics*, reports that by 1900 there were 25 dramatic critics on New York daily and weekly papers. Among these newspapers were several designed solely for the profession — *The New York Clipper, The Spirit of the Times, The Dramatic Mirror, The New York Dramatic News, Byrne's Dramatic Times,* and *The Theatre.*[19]

Significantly, Miller concludes that by 1890 the theatre critic had the status of a professional,[20] and however we may argue about the word's qualitative meaning in theatre practice, Miller's work has established that at least as early as 1890 critics were a force in the theatre that could not be ignored.

In the Drydenesque lakeside symposium that serves as the introduction to his 1965 *American Drama and its Critics,* editor Alan Downer has one of his participants say, "I always wondered what would have happened to the New Theater movement if it had had to battle the critical principles of William Winter. Instead, it confronted a new breed of judges, who were prepared to create the climate of opinion, as Eric Bentley says, in which the playwrights could live."[21] Another participant in the discussion says:

> *The dramatic critics, some of them, were ahead of the playwrights. And since they were without the responsibilities or the burdens of the creative men of the theater, they were surprisingly in tune with the public, with the climate of opinion. They were missionaries from the audience to the entertainers. As much as anyone they were responsible for the renaissance of drama in the United States after the First World War.*[22]

Though certainly self-celebratory, these views of criticism from 1890 to 1910 are not incorrect because in William Dean Howells, Hamlin Garland, Walter Pritchard Eaton, and others, the New Theatre Movement found early proponents and supporters of its work. Whether these critics and their fellows really just chronicled or actually created public opinion it may well be impossible to determine.

What kind of drama was it that these powerful critics wanted to encourage? It was an American drama modeled after "the more advanced drama of Europe, especially the plays of Ibsen."[23] Some critics found the domestic drama laggard in taking up social questions (rather than domestic issues),[24] and many critics argued that realism alone was the "inevitable road," the only source of "dramatic salvation."[25] As these plays found the audience which Downer's symposiasts argued had prefigured the plays themselves, moderating voices were raised, for example James Gibbons Huneker, who remarked in 1921, "The New Movement is less a dramatic revolution than a filtration of modern motives into the theater. The Ibsen technique dates back to the inexhaustible Scribe, while the Norwegian leans heavily in the matter of the thesis play on Dumas fils."[26] Huneker's observations about Ibsen are well taken and now accepted, as we all have occasion to remind ourselves from time to time,[27] but moderation did not prevail in the new movement as it evolved from 1890 to 1910, and Huneker's distinction between genre and style was lost in the fracas that accompanied that evolution.

The distinction was, however, exceedingly important so far as the fate of melodrama was concerned. There is no universally accepted definition of melodrama, but thus far the view that melodrama observes poetic justice — good is rewarded and evil is punished or the play makes clear this "ought" to be the case — has not been seriously challenged.[28] The popularity of these plays in nineteenth century American theatre is amply substantiated by the repertories of virtually every stock company in the country. Prior to 1890, as Tice Miller has observed, audiences no less than critics "were shaped by a society which valued a romantic and idealized art."[29] In this art, society functioned as it ought to and, conversely, it was the stated and accepted duty of melodrama, the theatre's most popular dramatic form throughout the nineteenth century, to carry out Horace's edict to teach morality. Clearly, however, by 1910 teaching alone was not enough. Nothing about the genre melodrama had changed, but its nineteenth century style had, as Lillian Mortimer observed, "outlived itself." Melodrama had met "naturalism."[30]

The nature of and critical responses to this seemingly straight forward interaction are far from simple. For one thing, advocates of the "new" drama and its accoutrements (directors, designers, etc.) and their disciples have contributed to a view of nineteenth century melodrama as, at best, quaint or amusing, but artistically contemptible. Recent scholarship has suggested a different view which sheds light upon the contributions of nineteenth century melodrama to the "new theatre movement," such contributions as a concern with politics, religion, sex, and other social issues, the advancement of verisimilitude in the mise-en-scène, and the life-like depiction of major characters from all — but especially the lower — social classes through dialect, dress, occupations, and habitat.[31] When we add to this inheritance the traditions of plot construction from the well-made play, then the new drama begins to assume a reasonable place in theatrical history. What remains is to correct the notion, articulated by James A. Herne and many since, that the New Theatre Movement triumphed despite popular indifference and in the face of critical opposition.

The question "was the public indifferent to the new drama" lies within the realm of theatre's economic history, a kingdom outside the boundaries of the present discussion. Until the question is addressed systematically, we can only point to effects and hazard educated guessed about causes. For example, the fall off in patronization of popular priced melodrama reported by Lillian Mortimer and reviewers occuring without a decrease in the popularity of "society" melodrama seems to point to a lack of audience interest in one style of theatrical melodrama — a mainstay of films at the time — rather than a widescale desertion of the genre. Moreover, a fair amount of that "society" melodrama *was* the new drama and it was commercially successful. We may argue whether *Rosmersholm* is melodrama or tragedy, but we can agree when Mrs. Fiske tells us she played it for "one hundred and ninety-nine consecutive performances at a profit of $40,000"[32] that the public was not indifferent. The 1890-1910 period provides numerous examples of the commercial success of other "new" or "naturalistic" plays, even those by American authors, many if not most of which we would not argue about calling melodramas. Granted, Lillian Mortimer's work suffered from the general decline of combinations on the road (down from 500 in 1900 to an average of 198 in 1910-14), yet melodramas in other styles continued to profit as the number of new plays in New York increased (up from an average of 72 in 1900-04 to 124 in 1915-19).

Did the "new" or "naturalistic" drama triumph in the face of opposition by critics, as Herne and his successors maintained, or was there a critical bias in favor of "new" or "naturalistic" drama, as Downer's symposiasts and I, though for different reasons, maintain? Certainly some critics were opposed to at least some of the new repertory. William Winter did call *Ghosts* "nauseous offal" in 1894 and Arnold Daly was brought to court in 1905 for producing such "immoral garbage" as *Mrs. Warren's Profession.*[33] In addition, there were then as there are now self-styled decency leagues, critics who supported them, and politicians who were prepared to go as far as censorship in their search for votes. Because the language of opposition to the "new" drama was expressive of moral rather than aesthetic opinions — "nauseous offal" and "immoral garbage" have, after all, nothing to say about the art of a play or the lack of it — and because the doctrine of poetic justice in melodrama seemed to satisfy the moral requirements of those opposed to the "new" drama, it was easy for the casually or personally involved theatre-goer to conclude that "new" dramas triumphed despite critical opposition and that they were the artistic opposite of melodrama. The first is a half truth and the second I believe to be false.

I have already cited Howells, Garland, and Eaton as professional critics of considerable influence who supported the work of the "New Theatre Movement." We might array them on one side and Winter and John Rankin Towse on the other and stage a battle of the super critics, but production reviewers may well be more indicative than these men of the kind of critic likely to have an influence on a play's popularity, and I have said that the remarkable thing in all this was that critics helped establish a change in audience taste. What the reviewers did was blur the distinction between genre and style in their reviews in such a way that they provided major support for the "new" or "naturalistic" drama by assigning artistic virtue to it and artistic vice to melodrama. As a result, melodrama lost the status of dramatic art, a fate from which it has not been finally rescued perhaps because our genre distinctions are not yet sufficiently detailed or generally accepted to allow us to readily agree that many of the "new" or "naturalistic" plays are and always have been melodramas, despite the ease with which one can prove the "new" drama and melodrama share many stylistic characteristics.

The shift in reviews follows a pattern. In the 1890's, it begins to matter to critics whether a melodrama has naturalistic/realistic elements, and critical language joins the terms melodrama and naturalistic/realistic. For example, Edward Dithmar reviewing Herne's *Margaret Fleming* (1891) for the *New York Times* listed among its merits that "it is realistic. We see human beings as they really are."[34] "Dramatic realism," said the *(Boston) Journal* of Herne's *Shore Acres* in 1893,[35] and a "truthful representation of New England life and characters" added the *Boston Times.*[36] Of Augustus Thomas' *Arizona* (1899/1900) the critic for the *Dramatic Mirror* says it is "melodrama of the highest and best type," with dialogue that is "easy and natural" and with well-drawn characters,[37] comments made about Thomas' earlier plays *Alabama* (1891) and *In Missoura* (1893). In addition to Herne and Thomas, whose plays are usually cited as examples of the "new" drama from the 1890's, numerous plays by melodramatists with no claims to "new drama" status are reviewed and evaluated positively in the 1890's in naturalistic terms and language, such as "realism," "accurate observation," "truth to life," "natural," and praised as works of quality. While it is true that by 1900 the beauties of a given melodrama, according to reviewers, are those which are considered naturalistic and which raise the play above those shortcomings of melodrama considered by reviewers to be traditional, it was also the case that plays with these characteristics were regarded by critics as good melodrama, good native drama, and good art.

In the decade from 1900 to 1910, when the majority of the American "new" dramatists — Sheldon, Fitch, Moody, Mackaye, Thomas — were writing (or writing the majority of their "new" dramas), the word melodrama emerges in reviews as a negative critical term. The faults of a play are equated with melodramatic elements, the virtues with naturalistic/realistic elements. For example, *Theatre Magazine* commended the "uncommon realism" of Sheldon's *Salvation Nell* (1908), its "true to life" acting, and scenes that were "full of reality."[38] More specifically, John Corbin said of *The Great Divide* (1906) in the *New York Sun* that it was "unusual and sensational in the manner not of melodrama, but of true and original drama. . . . A story which seems destined to melodrama and the false heroics of sentiment is treated with simplicity," and, finally, that "it all happens so much more naturally and subtly . . . no word rises above the utmost austerity of realism."[39] This language also appears in reviews of Moody's *Faith Healer* (1909). The *New York Tribune* said of Fitch's *The City* (1909), "If ever there were a powerful American play, firm and deft in construction, daring in plan, bold, frank, convincing, worthy to stand with much of the best work of the modern dramatists of the old world, this is that play."[40] The *Morning World* added the play was "sensationalism in its most virulent form, but it rang true."[41]

The idea that a play's faults were due to its genre had been illustrated as early as 1893 when the critic of the *Dramatic Mirror* said of Belasco's and Fyles' *The Girl I Left behind Me* that "events fall out too conveniently for the playwright's purpose, and not sufficiently in accord with the ways of nature. But . . . these details are not salient in a drama of melodramatic tendencies."[42] Examples of critics equating faults with melodrama and virtues with naturalistic/realistic elements abound in reviews of "gun and knife" melodramas from 1900 to 1910: the *Times* critic says of Wister's and LaShelle's *The Virginian* (1904) that western melodrama is not "a first rate art form," yet in this "melodrama realism and quietude unite, and the force of accurate observation and veracious emotions — prime qualities in the artistic drama" — raise this play to that level;[43] a critic of *The Girl of the Golden West* (1905) says it "is melodrama — but it is tense, moving, absorbing melodrama," with characters that "seem true to life" and "realistic" scenes;[44] a critic of *Billy the Kid* (1906) says the dialogue contains "the stock phrases of melodrama," but adds that the "comedy is natural, the characters resemble real people;"[45] and, finally, to turn to the greatest "gun and knife" melodrama of them all, the *Dramatic Mirror* says of *The Great Divide* that its author takes the "time-honored materials of melodrama" and produces "a drama that . . . rises far above the mere theatric effectiveness of melodrama."[46] Thus, by 1910, it was a contradiction in critical terms for the genre melodrama to be good theatre without the style naturalism.

There is nothing new about using terms like "realistic," "natural," "true to life," and similar words in reviews, for these have been parts of the critical vocabulary of praise since at least the eighteenth century, but it is a new idea in critical history, I think, to condemn a genre on the basis of these stylistic criteria. Though sometimes inconsistent and ambiguous, the language of reviews repeatedly speaks of a true and original drama, of an artistic modern European drama worthy of emulation, of a melodrama unconcerned with nature and "merely" theatrically effective. By 1910, melodrama was something the best plays rose above by being naturalistic or realistic and thereby either legitimizing sensationalism or suppressing melodramatic tendencies believed to be inherent in the form.

In summary, then, melodrama has survived the muddying of critical waters caused by indiscriminate use of generic and stylistic criteria, but it has not survived with its artistic reputation intact. This fate can, I have argued, be traced to a change in public taste which critics helped establish in the years between 1890 and 1910 when, in their desire to support a "new" style in playwriting they both purposively and unwittingly contributed to the demise of another style. That the results of this interaction is of more than erudite concern is borne out by the economic facts examplified in the declining popularity of Lilliam Mortimer's melodramas and melodrama company. Indeed, in her work and career can be seen an important shift in theatrical history reflective of a number of changes accompanying or wrought by the New Theatre Movement and "naturalism."

NOTES

[1]Unidentified Aug. 6, 1904, clipping in the N.Y.P.L. Mortimer wrote a play for each season during these years. Her 1904-05 entry was *Girl of the Streets* and her most popular play, *No Mother to Guide Her*, was the choice for 1905-06.

[2]"Lillian Mortimer Tells Why," *Variety*, Jan. 28, 1909.

[3]Arthur Knight, *The Liveliest Art* (N.Y.: New American Library, 1957), p. 55.

[4]These movie houses were also, at 25¢ (Strand), more expensive.

[5]Unidentified review of *A Girl's Best Friend* in the clipping file for Mortimer in the N.Y.P.L. Mortimer was fortunate to be able to escape to vaudeville for 20 years, though the sound film helped finish her second career there, just as the spectacular action silents had helped finish her melodrama company earlier.

[6]"Only Woman Author-Actor-Manager," *New York Telegraph*, July 10, 1904.

[7]*New York Telegraph*, July 15, 1906.

[8]"Only Woman Author-Actor-Manager."

[9]Unidentified review of *No Mother to Guide Her*, Dec. 17, 1905, from the clipping file, N.Y.P.L.

[10]"Only Woman Author-Actor-Manager."

[11]*Pittsburgh Post*, April 4, 1907.

[12]Ibid.

[13]*New York Telegraph,* Nov. 22, 1908.
[14]"Lillian Mortimer Tells Why," and "Faith in Melodrama," *Detroit News,* Feb. 19, 1913.
[15]"Faith in Melodrama."
[16]"Sees Melo Returning," *Columbus Dispatch,* Nov. 26, 1916.
[17]Unidentified review of *A Girl's Best Friend* in the Mortimer clipping file, N.Y.P.L.
[18]"Lillian Mortimer Tells Why."
[19]Tice Miller, *Bohemians and Critics: American Theatre Criticism in the Nineteenth Century* (Metuchen, N.J.: Scarecrow, Press, 1981), pp. 160-161.
[20]Ibid., p. 162.
[21]Alan S. Downer (ed.), *American Drama and Its Critics* (Chicago: Univ. of Chicago Press, 1965), p. xv.
[22]Ibid.
[23]Walter Pritchard Eaton, "Our Infant Industry" (1908), in Downer, p. 21.
[24]William Dean Howells, "Some New American Plays" (1904), in Downer, p. 10.
[25]Eaton, in Downer, p. 28.
[26]James Gibbons Huneker, "David Belasco" (1921), in Downer, p. 38.
[27]In my case, "The Influence of the Received Tradition upon Ibsen and His Reforms of It, with Illustrations from *A Doll House,*" a presentation for the Ohio State University Lecture Series, Feb. 28, 1981.
[28]I have articulated the position, but am neither the first nor only person to have done so, in "The Nature of Melodrama," presented as part of the Competitive Panel in Theory and Criticism at the A.T.A. National Convention in 1979, and "The Ethical and the Artistic: Melodrama As A Dirty Word," presented as part of the Debut Panel at the S.C.A. National Convention in 1976.
[29]Miller, p. 162.
[30]This interaction has been discussed in a limited way in my "Melodrama Meets Naturalism: Critical Receptions of the American Frontier Play, 1890-1910," a presentation for the Debut Panel at the A.T.A. National Convention in 1976.
[31]See Michael R. Booth's "A Defence of Nineteenth-Century English Drama," in *ETJ,* vol. 26, no. 1 (March, 1974), pp. 5-13.
[32]Alexander Woollcott, *Mrs. Fiske: Her Views on the Stage* (rpt. 1917; New York: Benjamin Blom, 1968), p. 47.
[33]Shaw was, of course, delighted to have his view of social oppression confirmed, though Daly was acquitted.
[34]*New York Times,* Dec. 10, 1891.
[35]*(Boston) Journal,* Feb. 21, 1893.
[36]*(Boston) Times,* Feb. 26, 1893.
[37]*(New York) Dramatic Mirror,* Sept. 15, 1900, p. 17.
[38]*Theatre Magazine,* January, 1908.
[39]*New York Sun,* Oct. 4, 1906.
[40]*New York Tribune,* Dec. 22, 1909.
[41]*Morning World,* Dec. 22, 1909.
[42]*Dramatic Mirror,* Feb. 4, 1893, p. 11.
[43]*New York Times,* Jan. 6, 1904, p. 2.
[44]*New York Times,* Nov. 15, 1905, p. 13.
[45]*Dramatic Mirror,* Aug. 25, 1906, p. 8.
[46]Ibid., Oct. 13, 1906, p. 3.

Gémier and Baty's *La Grande Pastorale*: a Medieval Mystery Play for the Twentieth Century

Langdon Brown

Firmin Gémier, who began his theatrical career with Antoine's Théâtre-libre, was famous for experiments designed to attract working class people to the theatre. I have discussed two such experiments elsewhere,[1] including his 1919 spectacle, *Oedipe roi de Thèbes*, staged at the Cirque d'Hiver in Paris. Having pursued the creation of a new popular theatre and drama based on Greek and medieval historical models in that production, Gémier moved to a more specialized reliance on the medieval model in his second and final circus production, *La Grande Pastorale*. Another Gémier experiment, the Théâtre National Ambulant, had brought the Paris theatre to the provinces in 1910 and 1911; in 1920, he reversed the process to bring a traditional form of provincial drama to Paris.

Although *La Grande Pastorale* was Gémier's concept, the execution of the production was left to his recently acquired lieutenant, who was later to earn more lasting fame than Gémier himself: Gaston Baty. During the period following the First World War, Gémier's career burgeoned and it is not difficult to understand his search for a trustworthy subordinate. He managed the Théâtre Antoine until 1922; he launched the Cirque d'Hiver experiment and starred in *Oedipe* in 1919; he campaigned to found and direct a fourth national theatre, the Théâtre National Populaire in 1920; he entered the "art theatre" market with a season at the Comédie Montaigne (Comédie des Champs Elysées) in 1920-21; and he successfully fought to obtain the directorship of the Odéon in 1922. Thus it is not surprising that when he was approached by the young Baty in April of 1919, Gémier gratefully noted the talent evident in the promptbooks Baty submitted for his perusal and signed him to a contract as "director in the theatres under my management now or in the future, for a period of five years beginning September 1 [1919]."[2]

Baty thus began his theatrical career at thirty-three after spending his early years in his family's lumber business near Lyon. It is characteristic that Baty placed his duty to his family before his personal goals. He was partially compensated for his altruism with business trips permitting him to study a variety of European theatrical traditions. Impressed particularly by what he saw in Germany, he decided to educate himself as a complete theatre artist and, before being called to military duty in the First World War, he studied and wrote plays and theoretical tracts. Gémier moved his company

Langdon Brown is Chairman of the Department of Theatre at the University of Bridgeport. He has published articles on Gémier in *Theatre Journal* and *Theatre Survey*.

Opening scene of *La Grande Pastoral,* "A Farm Courtyard". Photo courtesy Bibliothéque Nationale, Département des Arts du Spectacle, Collection G. Baty.

to Lyon during the 1918 bombardment of Paris and met Baty there in April, 1919.[3]

Baty and Gémier derived great mutual benefit from their association. Each had developed a philosophy of theatre art based on service to mankind and they agreed on the need for productions both visually attractive and intellectually accessible. Gémier needed someone with the time and inclination to deal with detail and the consolidation of his ambitious projects. Baty, a thoughtful, thorough student of the theatre, was capable of faith in the visionary Gémier. Baty concentrated his efforts where Gémier dispersed his, and while Gémier benefited from Baty's extensive knowledge and dedication to the finer points of stagecraft, Baty learned a great deal about directing actors from his apprenticeship with Gémier.

Gémier first tested Baty as lighting designer for *Oedipe,* and Baty won widespread notice and praise from the critics. Gémier immediately entrusted the entire *mise-en-scéne* of *La Grande Pastorale* to Baty, despite a scale of production almost as grand as that of the *Oedipe*. The non-Parisian Baty was the right one to accomplish the project's goal, which was to use the dramatic traditions of the provinces to revitalize French drama. Gémier, like Romain Rolland and the adherents of the *théâtre du peuple* movement, advocated reform of the drama, but unlike them, he despaired of attempts to invent a new dramatic form through manifestoes and appeals to the Parisian dramatic establishment. Instead, Gémier proposed a conscientious examination of the popular folkloric tradition of the entire nation. He thought French history might supply a mythic foundation for a new theatre, a theatre like that of ancient Greece. Gémier rejected traditional biographical history, however, while advocating contemplation of the collective life of the masses: "It would be well to study . . . the life of the people, their suffering, their revolutions, the sufferings of their forgotten champions, their terrible fits of sudden ferocity, the wonderful outpourings of their generous instincts."[4] Such theatre could examine a phenomenon central to the history of France: mob psychology. Given Gémier's talent for staging crowd scenes, such a theatre would confront French audiences with an essential trait of the national character. But it was not only the Parisian mob that deserved attention; Gémier insisted that untapped wealth was to be found in provincial tradition:

> *Think of the thousand entertaining and tragic stories one could glean from our old provinces. Doesn't each have its own favorite heroes, its traditional garb, its songs, its dances, its caps, and its wimples? Doesn't each one have its legends that harbor its soul? Just imagine the rich cycle that could be composed from these diverse yet harmonious traditions, the sumptuous garland one could weave around the nation's altar with all the indiginous flowers from the Vosges to the Pyrenees, from the Alps to the Atlantic. Thus we would pay tribute to the regional virtues which together formed the character of the nation, and we would impart a new vigor to them to activate them in today's society.*
>
> *So you can see an almost unused and unlimited source in to-*

Scene two of *La Grande Pastoral,* "Hell". Photo courtesy Bibliothéque Nationale, Département des Arts du Spectacle, Collection G. Baty.

day's social life, in history, and in provincial legends. It is said that our authors are afraid to test these sources. Yet in them teem the thoughts and images that could instruct the modern public.[5]

To achieve this dream, Gémier planned to follow the success of *Oedipe* with a series of "Spectacles de la Vielle France" at the Cirque d'Hiver. The series would present the representative dramatic traditions of the provinces. The first, *La Grand Pastorale,* would represent Provence, where devout faith and the long survival of the medieval tradition of mystery plays had left a dramatic style susceptible to immediate modern use. Gémier asked two authors from the region, Pol d'Estoc and Charles Hellem, to create such a drama for the premiére of this series.

Gémier specified that the play should not be so regionalized in dialect as to be incomprehensible to the Parisian audience, but rather should appeal more for freshness and originality than for local color. Gémier had no desire to war against the current modes of drama, but rather to add to the options available to playwrights.

In coming to the Cirque d'Hiver, we began our escape from "Modern Theatre." Our program leads us towards the collective theatre, the national theatre. Our ideas hold nothing against the popular genres. But it is certainly reasonable to think that after the war where all social classes found themselves side by side in the misery of the trenches, the theatre should be accessible to all, the way it was years ago in the festivals that gathered all in a public place or the cathedral square to taste the joys of primitive spectacles. They term this theatre popular or national. I term it collective.

Dramatic art for all requires sound plays whose composition and content must create enthusiasm among common men and the elite.[6]

The socialist Gémier thought in terms of an international brotherhood of people united in a common notion of ethics, decency, and enlightened self-interest. A first step toward that goal was the unification of the French people who, Gémier claimed, were badly divided, with Paris practically ignoring the rest of the country:

Because of centralization, Paris seems to be disconnected from its familial ties with the rest of France. As a result, the provinces always show the same infatuation with what the capital exports. They go so far as to discard their own picturesque caps for those awful hats from the cheap stores. The traditional songs are set aside in favor of the gags from the café-concert. The ornaments and toys of the mountains or the plains are forsaken for trinkets from Paris, which just as often aren't from Paris, or even from France. Dare I say that in Paris one often feels that he is no longer in France. In reality, the French ignore each other. If they confronted each other more often, if they knew themselves better, they

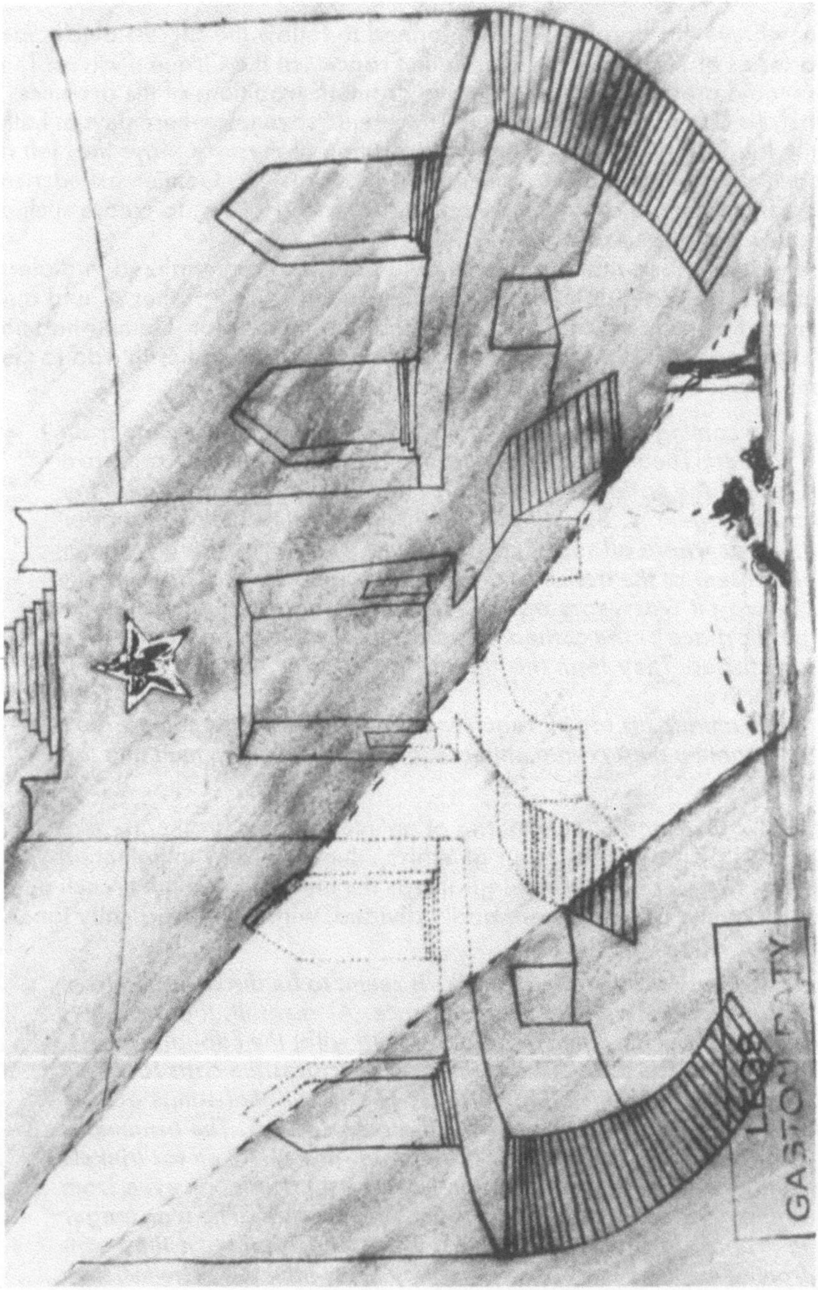

The shepherds receive the "good news" scene in *La Grande Pastoral*. Photo courtesy Bibliothéque Nationale, Département des Arts du Spectacle, Collection G. Baty.

> *would like each other more. Why not provoke such confrontations?*[7]

Gémier's vision did not stop with the unification of the French. He looked beyond the "Spectacles de la Vielle France" to the day when theatrical performances would reach the proportions of the festivals of the French Revolution, on an international scale, speaking to, and uniting, all classes:

> *I will give other neighboring spectaculars with musical and sporting themes, scholarly festivals, and craftsmen's spectacles. Thus the theatre will return to its origins, becoming again a popular festival. It will rediscover its grandeur in returning to collectivity.*[8]

While Gémier dreamed of the future, Pol d'Estoc, Charles Hellem, and Baty dealt with the more immediate concerns of adapting the age-old pastoral form to the requirements of Gémier's circus stage. They explained:

> *All the traditional characters were included: shepherds, farmhands, gypsies, etc. Our pastoral will not differ from those played in Provence for 150 years, every year at Christmas, which are a remnant of the mystery plays of the Middle Ages.*[9]

The typical plot of a "pastorale" concerned the reunion of a Provençal father and his prodigal son before Christ in the manger. The culprit was a gypsy punished with blindness for her crime and later converted and cured. Variants have angels appearing to Provençal shepherds, pageants of Provençal and Biblical characters making the journey to Bethlehem, and subplots revolving around calamities befalling village inhabitants which are remedied with the coming of Christ. The authors explained the simple morality, a feature central to Gémier's concept, as a sacrament in a nondenominational civic religion:

> *Pastorals, performed only by countryfolk, reflect the mores of the rural locale in such a particularly exact way that, in each, a domestic drama of "local color" follows the nativity play. Daudet's* L'Arlesienne[10] *is a traditional domestic drama that derives from this tradition. The conflict pits the forces of good against the forces of evil, one represented by the family and the virgin bride, and the other by the "bouhmiano," the black gypsy, who tries to seduce the bridegroom. Needless to say, the forces of evil succumb to the assaults of the forces of good and the end result (no half measures here!) is the conversion of the whole Satanic tribe, the gypsy included.*[11]

One critic previewed Gémier's new project while expressing hope that Gémier would not compromise the simplicity and quaint piety of the form by altering it to suit Parisian tastes.[12]

Hellem and d'Estoc's play opened in the courtyard of a farm in the Midi where a large group of Provençals celebrated the impending marriage of

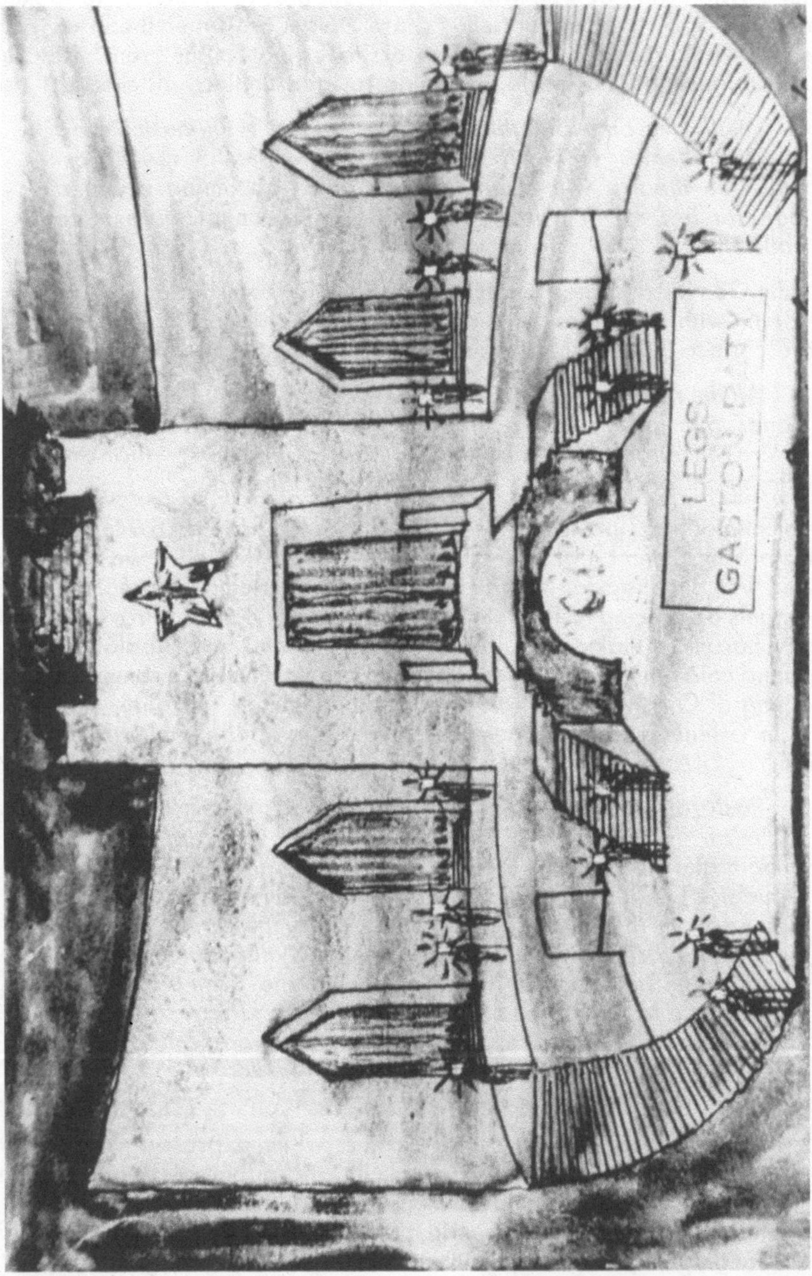

Final scene of *La Grande Pastoral* in Bethlehem. Photo courtesy Bibliothèque Nationale, Département des Arts du Spectacle, Collection G. Baty.

Micolou and Flouette. As the characters were introduced, a dance wound around, off, and back on stage, preserving the spectacular tone of the preceding production of *Oedipe*. The plot thickened with the arrival of a group of gypsies camped near the farm, who were allowed to join the festivities (with a dancing bear in tow) against the warnings of a wise old shepherd who perceived their evil nature. Despite further warnings, Micolou's head was turned by a gypsy dancer, whose gyrations were interrupted by a series of catastrophes not intended to be taken too seriously, including the burning of the farm, Micolou's disappearance, the loss of sanity of one of Micolou's brothers, and the visitation of an attack of uncontrollable stammering on another. The burning farm scene dissolved into a fiery hell, complete with roasting sinners, parades of the damned, Satan, and the seven deadly sins.

After an *entr'acte* the scene shifted to the fields where the wise old shepherd discussed the disaster with his fellows, until the star of Bethlehem and an angel interrupted with the traditional Christmas announcement to the accompaniment of a choir of extras singing *Gloria*. The old shepherd rounded up the rest of the cast, leading them in pursuit of the star through the orchestra in search of the birthplace of Christ. Their journey wound out of the house and back on stage where Mary and Joseph as well as the gypsy dancer (now a leper) awaited them. After a final exit through another part of the auditorium there followed another *entr'acte*.

In the final two scenes the travelers came to the young Judas Iscariot's lodgings, where they were treated to the most spectacular scene in the play: a parade of the three kings. Finally they reached the manger, where all worshipped and offered gifts. There followed a number of happy miracles, including the restoration of sight to a fellow traveler, the reformation of a gypsy, and the cure of the stammering and idiot brothers. The gypsy dancer, however, unrepentant to the end, was consigned to hell.

Scenes such as the parade of the kings illustrate Gémier and Baty's emphasis on visual spectacle. In the parade scene, the kings of Africa, Asia, and Europe led a retinue totalling 82 actors across the stage in a dancing procession of gift bearers, slaves, warriors, Hindus, idols, witch doctors, pages, archers, and dancers. Apparently, audiences of the time found the black members of this company particularly exotic, and their entrance never failed to elicit a round of applause. The importance of visual elements to this production was another good argument for Gémier's heavy reliance on Baty, whose renderings for the production prefigure the later successes he was to enjoy in the manipulation of light and scenery.[13] It seems clear from the promptbook in Baty's hand in the Bibliothèque de l'Arsenal that the structure of the production came from Gémier, and the visual dressing from Baty.

The play's religious theme was another good reason for the religiously ambivalent Gémier to turn to the devoutly Catholic Baty. Journalists' accounts of rehearsals indicate, however, that Gémier maintained the last word in artistic decisions, and they rarely mention Baty, although this is partially because Gémier was at the height of his fame and made excellent copy. Hellem's recollection helps to establish that the direction of *La Grande*

Pastorale was a collaborative effort with Gémier benefiting from Baty's complete job of planning the production as evidenced by the promptbook, and Baty benefiting from the corrections and advice of Gémier:

> *The actors understood very well that the true authority came from "The boss," which is to say, Gémier. Baty needed a great deal of patience, diplomacy, and graciousness to obtain the results he wanted. But he displayed a wealth of tenacity, which explains, in part, the success of his career.*[14]

Hellem's recollection of another specific incident illustrates the dynamic of the relationship and the actors' occasional difficulties with the inexperienced Baty:

> *Around the middle of the rehearsal Gémier arrived and sat down in one of the orchestra seats. Then, all of a sudden, he got up and jumped up on stage, his hat pushed back on his head. . . . He went over the business Baty had worked out, corrected an intonation, explained and justified the reason for his choice, and then turned the direction back to his collaborator, to the mute delight of certain of the actors.*[15]

Still there was no doubt about Gémier's estimation of the magnitude of Baty's contribution, as Hellem noted: "Gémier, who also put all of the resources of his immense talent into the production of *La Grande Pastorale*, recognized without prompting Baty's contribution to the preparation of our play, and loyally, generously, he listed Baty as director on the poster and in the program."[16] Despite this, critics referred almost exclusively to the *mise en scéne* of Gémier, and at the preview, when Baty was announced as the *metteur en scéne,* the loudest applause was saved for the charismatic Gémier.

All of this does not seem to have distracted Baty from giving his best effort. He built upon the solid foundation of the *Oedipe* success, using the same team of designers and technicians. For economic reasons, Baty designed a set utilizing the structure already in place for the *Oedipe,* a circular area split in half between the audience and the playing area. In that set five broad steps running the full width of the arena led from the orchestra level to the first playing level, around which curved the Theban palace. An immense central stairway dominated the setting, leading up to the simple and massive palace facade, pierced by one large central opening and four smaller openings on the two wings. The main structural change from this *Oedipe* set was "a new arrangement of the central stairway, under which was placed a recess. . . ."[17] In place of the grand central staircase of *Oedipe* was a double set of stairs giving access to a central platform at the same height as the level in front of the palace facade, which was now partially neutralized by a covering of white crepe rendered different colors by varied lighting in the six tableaux of the play. Scene changes were accomplished with lighting as well as changes in the curtains hung in the openings of the facade. In the first scene, a farm and courtyard were represented by partially obscuring the facade with a large tree, bleaching the remaining walls with white light, and hanging a temporary roof on the sides of the facade. This scene was changed in a blackout to the second tableau of hell by removing the tree, the roof, and the curtains in the openings of the facade. Blue light focused on the facade contrasted with fiery drops placed in the stage right and the stage left openings of the facade, and in the bay under the central platform, while the large central opening became a hellmouth, complemented by nostrils and eyes higher on the central facade. The balance of the scenes was created by adding a star on the upper part of the facade, spotlighting a straw-covered area on the lower level to look like a field, placing the manger in the central bay, and replacing the curtains in the openings of the facade with other curtains and, in one scene, with a vista of cypress trees.[18]

Baty suggested that the costumes of 17th-century Provençal peasants would provide the proper look for the production. He further recommended the paintings of Bosch and Callot as models for the damned in the second tableau of the descent into hell. He and Gémier arranged for H. M. Jacquet to adapt the country tunes of the South for incidental music as well as the Lully "Marche de Turenne" for the procession of the kings.[19]

Despite the spectacular production effects, and another heavy barrage of publicity, the popular success of *Oedipe* was not repeated. About half as many performances of *La Grande Pastorale* were presented as of the *Oedipe*, and the receipts, at 156,699 francs, were even less than half of those of the first production.[20] Thus, the popular verdict did not augur well for a continuation of Gémier's experiment at the Cirque d'Hiver.

The critical opinions, while not as heated as those excited by the *Oedipe*, were nonetheless generally favorable and continued the debate over spectacular versus literary productions. Typically, French reviewers reacted to the play by praising the spectacular effects and then sternly reminding Gémier of the importance of the literary pretext behind any scenic effort. Characteristic of judgment on the direction and design was Paul Abram's comment in *Le Théâtre*:

> *It would seem that Gémier has never more artistically achieved a composition of such a richness of colors, of such a harmony of tones. Each element appears to be arranged masterfully. It is a superb tableau of unusual proportions where the most delicate taste finds something to satisfy it. . . . Incessant applause and acclamation greeted this army of characters and costumes.*[21]

Judgments on the crowd scenes, which represented a more recognizable picture of everyday people pursuing normal tasks and pleasures than the politically obsessed Theban chorus of *Oedipe*, also were favorable, as again exemplified by Abram:

> *And the huge, turbulent, swarming crowd, streaming on the staircase or marching across the stage in a parade, gives an intense vitality to most of the scenes, while the lonely passage of Joseph and Mary, and the donkey, alone on the huge set, was*

> *like a peaceful, blue corner of the heavens stilling for a moment the storm of human passion.*[22]

The few critics who were unqualified in their praise tended to be those already favorably disposed toward the *théâtre du peuple* movement:

> *It is the pure reflection of the people's soul; just as the imagery of antiphonal responses and the saints on the altar, the scenes of the medieval theatre have preserved this great and delicate spirit, which both the most jaded man and the simplest child can equally enjoy.*[23]

Others tended to see the play as an excuse for dances and costumes and scenes such as the descent into hell, which gave a pretext for much the same kind of entertainment one would find in a music hall. *Le Figaro*'s Robert de Flers noted that the play came from a genre that promised much for the popular theatre, but that the authors neglected the necessary element of naiveté, diminishing the effect and purity of the production for either a literate or a popular audience:

> *. . . mysticism is too obviously used in the service of spectacle. It is a sort of puzzle, half secular, half sacred, where the sole artist is the director. He deserves all the praise he has received. The scene in hell is arrestingly horrifying. We viewed the grilling of the victims on huge fires, turned again and again by attentive demons who baste the criminals with huge spoons, according to the best culinary practice, while at the same time all sorts of little red and black demons tumble down the stairs with all the frenetic delight that in the theatre one sees only in the damned. The final tableau at the manger is one of harmonious magnificence. One must congratulate M. H. G. Ibels, who designed the costumes with taste and remarkable imagination. Those in the first scene, in which we see the festivities of the Provençal celebration, are of a marvelous brilliance and seem to bounce about in the sun of the Midi.*[24]

Another critic went even further to assert that neither the author nor the actor could find a place on a stage so overwhelmed with spectacle: ". . . this time, it is the actor, M. Gémier, who is himself expelled from a spectacle in which his subtle art and psychological playing cannot find a place among the tamborinists, tumblers and trained animals. . . . "[25] At the other end of the spectrum were critics who found Gémier's work without value and argued that he was simply seeking the lowest level of taste, and that far from moving toward a new theatre, he was debasing the one that existed:

> *. . . I reproached M. Gémier for having enslaved his play* Oedipe *in excessive spectacle: this time, he avoids any such objection by having taken the precaution, in his new production, of eliminating the play altogether. . . .*
>
> *As a result, if I try to define what Gémier has done in his new*

production, I would say that by means of a seductive, incontestable beauty, he has pushed theatre art to the point where he risks losing it altogether. We complain about the lack of plays; one could hope that by a natural reactive process, this void would itself spark new productivity and suggest encouraging new possibilities to the talented. However, Gémier just inaugurated the theater without a play: isn't that the coup de grâce.[26]

The issue of literary value versus scenic investiture was by no means resolved with the criticism of *La Grande Pastorale*. It was a controversy Baty would address throughout his career, especially after his essay entitled *Sire le Mot*, in which he argued against the primacy of the text. Curiously, André Antoine felt that Gémier and Baty did not incorporate enough spectacle into the play, in the sense that changeable scenery would have freed them to deal more ingeniously with those parts of the play where its language did not support its illusions.

For Baty, the production marked a successful debut and pointed the way to his focus on the non-verbal elements of theatre art. For Gémier the production's results were more complicated. His ideal of founding a permanent popular theatre was temporarily frustrated and it seemed clear that he could not hope to establish a *théâtre du peuple* using only his own resources. Only a subsidy could ensure a popular theatre's solvency until theatre-going became a habit for the lower classes, and then continued subsidy would be needed to ensure maintenance of affordable ticket prices. Just as clear was the popular audience's demand for spectacle, and for a star of Gémier's magnitude in addition to an entertaining play. The economics of the Cirque d'Hiver persuaded Gémier to seek public support for the Théâtre National Populaire, and its establishment in 1920 owed a great deal to the publicity and public awareness created by the Cirque d'Hiver experiment. So although the Cirque d'Hiver experiment was not totally successful, it provided the basis for France's first nationally subsidized popular theatre. Although Gémier was ahead of his time and his Théâtre National Populaire did not fulfill its potential in his lifetime, the idea and the institution endured until the vision and artistry of Jean Vilar, Georges Wilson, and Roger Planchon moved the Théâtre National Populaire into the front rank of the world's theatres.

NOTES

1Langdon Brown, "Firmin Gémier's Cirque d'Hiver production of *Oedipe roi de Thèbes*," *Theatre Journal*, 31 (October, 1979), 370-85; and "Firmin Gémier's Théâtre National Ambulant," *Theatre Survey*, 21 (May, 1980), 33-48.

2Paul Blanchart, *Firmin Gémier* (Paris: L'Arche, 1954), p. 178. All translations are my own.

3Clement Borgal, *Metteurs en Scène* (Paris: Fernand Lancre, 1963), pp. 133-39; Paul Blanchart, "Gaston Baty, notes et documents biographiques et bibliographiques," *Revue d'Histoire du Théâtre*, 5 (1953), 12-17.

4Firmin Gémier, *Le Théâtre* (Paris: Bernard Grasset, 1923), p. 210.

5Gémier, *Théâtre*, pp. 211-12.

6Firmin Gémier, "Spectacles de la Vielle France," *Comoedia* (March 9, 1920), in Collection Rondel, Bibliothèque de l'Arsenal.

7Gémier, "Spectacles."

[8]Gémier, "Spectacles."

[9]Quoted in F. Vignard, "*La Grande Pastorale,* Les auteurs MM. Ch. Ellen [sic] et Pol d'Estoc nous confient leurs projets," in Collection Rondel, Bibliothèque de l'Arsenal.

[10]One of the plays in the repertory of the Théâtre National Ambulant Gémier.

[11]Vignard, "*Grande Pastorale.*"

[12]Edmond Jaloux, "La Pastorale á Paris," unidentified clipping in Collection Rondel, Bibliothèque de l'Arsenal.

[13]Gaston Baty and Firmin Gémier, Promptbook of *La Grande Pastorale,* Fonds Gaston Baty, Bibliothèque de l'Arsenal, Collections des Arts du Spectacle.

[14]Quoted in Blanchart, *Gémier,* p. 223.

[15]Quoted in Blanchart, *Gémier,* p. 224.

[16]Quoted in Blanchart, *Gémier,* p. 224.

[17]Baty and Gémier, Promptbook.

[18]Baty and Gémier, Promptbook.

[19]Vignard, "*Grande Pastorale.*"

[20]Cited in Blanchart, *Gémier,* p. 227.

[21]Paul Abram, Untitled review of *La Grande Pastorale, Le Théâtre,* 381 (n.d.), 13, in Collection Rondel, Bibliotnèque de l'Arsenal.

[22]Abram, "*Grande Pastorale,*" p. 14.

[23]Henri Beraud, "Nouveau Voyage," unidentified clipping in Collection Rondel, Bibliothèque de l' Arsenal.

[24]Robert de Flers, "La Semaine Dramatique," *Le Figaro* (March 14, 1920), in Collection Rondel, Bibliothèque de l'Arsenal.

[25]Gaston de Pawlowski, "*La Grande Pastorale,*" (March 11, 1920) in Collection Rondel Bibliothèque de l'Arsenal.

[26]Gaston Rageot, "Le Théâtre: Le décor sans pièce et la pièce sans décor," *Revue Bleu,* 58 (March 27, 1920), 189-90.

Ibsen's Women Characters and Their Feminist Contemporaries

KATHERINE HANSON

In a speech addressed to the Norwegian Women's Rights League in 1898, Henrik Ibsen declined the honor that those emancipated women wished to bestow upon him with these words:

> *I must disclaim the honor of having consciously worked for the emancipation of women. I am not, in fact, entirely sure what women's emancipation really is; my concern has been with the emancipation of people.*[1]

This oft-quoted statement has been construed to mean that Ibsen was not a champion of women's rights, but that is hardly the case. In the first place, Ibsen did, on more than one occasion, demand that laws be changed so as to grant women greater freedom and equality. In 1879, in an impassioned speech to the members of the Scandinavian Society in Rome, Ibsen urged that the position of librarian be filled by a woman and, furthermore, that women in the Society be given the right to vote. The latter suggestion was met with great opposition and Ibsen was reportedly so enraged that he refused to frequent the society or associate with its members for quite some time. Five years later, in 1884, the Norwegian Storting received a document from authors Bjørnstjerne Bjørnson, Henrik Ibsen, Jonas Lie and Alexander Kielland written in support of a petition demanding that married women be given the right to own property and, in more general terms, be awarded legal authority: "The woman must know and feel, that she is entering into marriage with the same legal rights as the man" and ". . . it is in the interest of society that a married woman ceases to be legally incompetent."[2]

But even apart from these instances where Ibsen actively took a stand, it is still incorrect to interpret the statement that his concern has been the emancipation of people as an expression of disinterest in or estrangement from the affairs and conditions of women in society. For in its widest and most profound context, the emancipation of women is the emancipation of all human beings. And this is a belief that Ibsen not only shared with, but very likely learned from, the pioneers of the feminist movement in his native Norway, Camilla Collett and Aasta Hansteen. Like Ibsen, Collett and Hansteen understood the importance of rewriting laws to the greater freedom and protection of women, but they firmly believed that legal rights alone would not

Katherine Hanson has taught Norwegian language and literature at St. Olaf College and the University of Washington. She is currently editing and translating an anthology of short stories by Norwegian women writers to be published by the University of Minnesota Press.

free the individual, male or female, to pursue self-realization. In their writings these women advocated a spiritual emancipation; they demanded greater respect for women as women, for feminine abilities, feminine emotions — in a word, for the feminine personality.

Camilla Collett (b. 1813, d. 1895) has the double honor of being Norway's first feminist author and of writing the first realistic novel in Norwegian literature which critically discusses social issues and conditions. The novel, *The Governor's Daughters,* was published in parts in 1854-55 and it is a bitter attack on the institution of marriage with its total disregard of the woman's preference and feelings. Consequently, Collett tells the reader, real, genuine love is foreign to most marriages for it is in the spirit and soul of *woman* that love resides. That Ibsen read *The Governor's Daughters* goes without saying — during the 1850s Ibsen was intensely interested in creating and promoting a Norwegian literature and he undoubtedly read everything of importance that was published by a Norwegian author. That this novel made a deep impression on him is evidenced in *Love's Comedy* (1862). Ibsen's first drama in a contemporary setting, though still written in verse, *Love's Comedy* is a biting satire on marriage. The emphasis in character and plot is, quite naturally, different from *The Governor's Daughters,* but the sentiments are the same as in Collett's novel.

Ibsen continued to be influenced and inspired by Camilla Collett both through her writings and long conversations they had together. In his monumental work on Ibsen, Halvdan Koht tells of two occasions when Camilla Collett visited the Ibsens, once in Dresden in 1871 and again in Munich in 1877. They discussed marriage and the position of women in society, evidently with some vehemence, for we hear that Ibsen provoked Collett to anger with his old-fashioned and conservative views toward women. Koht suggests that this was a ploy Ibsen used, particularly during the 1877 visit, so that he might gain insight into the thoughts and feelings of a woman who was rebelling against the small-minded, hypocritical society of the bourgeoisie. Whether or not this was the case, Ibsen was most certainly affected by Collett's presence, for later on that same year he sent *Pillars of Society* to the publisher.

It was not, however, Camilla Collett who was Ibsen's chief model for Lona Hessel. That person was Aasta Hansteen who, though not nearly as articulate as Collett, was a more outspoken proponent of women's rights and has come to be known as the martyr of the Norwegian women's movement. Aasta Hansteen (b. 1824, d. 1908) was an accomplished portrait painter, but she abandoned that career in favor of working for causes. In 1874 she came to the defense of a Swedish baroness who claimed that she had been seduced by a Norwegian medical student who then refused to marry her. Hansteen saw this as an issue involving all women and she joined the baroness in demanding that the student be expelled from the University; she held speeches, she wrote articles, she organized demonstrations. This kind of activity was unheard of at the time and Aasta Hansteen became a public laughing stock. Ibsen was in Norway that summer, the first time in ten years, and he was as taken with the robust nature and undaunted spirit of this woman as he was indignant at the way she was mistreated by the public and by the press.

From the notes and early drafts of *Pillars of Society*, it is clear that Ibsen at one time intended for this play to deal much more explicitly with the issue of women's rights than it ultimately does. But as the play took form in Ibsen's mind, as the characters grew and developed, Lona Hessel assumed a much broader base than the timely issue of women's emancipation. In the play's closing lines, when Consul Bernick declares, "It is you women who are the pillars of society," Lona Hessel solemnly corrects him saying, "No, the spirit of truth and freedom — those are the pillars of society." This shift in emphasis, however, by no means lessens the impact these feminists had on Ibsen's writing, for the most important legacy of a woman like Aasta Hansteen was not ideas, but rather the heart, soul and personality of the character she gave rise to.

The indebtedness Ibsen owes Camilla Collett reaches further and deeper. He greatly esteemed this woman of remarkable talent and courage, and his admiration is freely expressed in letters he wrote to her. On the occasion of her seventieth birthday, 1883, he paid her this homage:

> *Ideas grow and propagate themselves slowly with us in the North; progress is unobservable; nevertheless it is made. The Norway now in process of development will bear traces of your intellectual pioneer-work. You are one of the fighters whom it will be most imperative for posterity to take into account in arriving at any understanding of that process.*[3]

That he too has been inspired by her "intellectual pioneer-work" is acknowledged in this letter from 1889: "But it is many years now since you, by virtue of your characteristic spiritual and intellectual development, began, in one form or another, to make your influence felt in my writings."[4]

Ibsen's attitude towards his feminist contemporaries, then, was clearly positive, but how did these women react to Ibsen and the women he created in the late 1870s and the decade that followed? In my reading I have come across a number of articles and reviews, written by women during the last quarter of the 19th century, all of them expressing enthusiasm and praise for the contribution Ibsen made to the creation of a new race of women. There were several women who, in the 1870s, started writing literary reviews in newspapers and magazines as well as longer critical works on literature that were published separately. These women belonged to an intellectual upper class where an active interest in literature had been cultivated for several generations. They were well versed in European literature, both classical and modern, and one would therefore expect them to be sophisticated critics.

In 1877 Camilla Collett published a book of essays, and among them is an article entitled "Woman in Literature. Native Authors." Ibsen is, of course, included, and Collett begins her discussion by pointing to his portrayal of self-sacrificing women — Agnes (*Brand*) and Solveig (*Peer Gynt*) are given as examples. Responding to her own question as to whether we should be moved by these figures, she emphatically says:

> *No, we will no longer be moved by that. Reluctantly we turn away from this wrinkled, careworn faithfulness, which has been sitting with folded hands, staring at one spot, waiting for — Peer Gynt, the old Peer Gynt — egoism in a state of decrepitude when, exhausted from its insatiability, it finally staggers home. And this melancholy figure here, it is not Solveig . . . it is our own dear, native born womanliness, which has outlived itself and now sits waiting for the sorcerer who with his wand will restore health and strength, and this sorcerer, this liberator, is none other than — Ibsen himself.*
>
> *Yes, Ibsen himself. What do you suppose he thought and felt when he conjured forth these pathetic shadows of womanhood — himself frightened by them?*
>
> *His works yet unwritten shall provide the answer.*[5]

Collett explains this optimistic expectancy regarding the women who were to emerge in Ibsen's later plays, with a brief reference to the strong and willful women in his very early saga dramas — Hjørdis (*The Vikings at Helgeland*) and Lady Inger (*Lady Inger of Østrat*) come immediately to mind — who, she reminds the reader, were enthusiastically greeted by herself and her sisters. These women could give themselves with abandon, but they also took; they were not passively obedient and self-effacing, but bold both in word and in deed. Collett must, however, have had more than these super-women from Norway's heroic past in mind, when she made these hopeful observations. Her prediction that Ibsen would step forth as sorcerer and liberator was undoubtedly based on her longtime association with the dramatist, the hours of heated discussion which, Collett was confident, had not been in vain.

As if in direct response to Collett's cry for liberation, *A Doll's House* was published in 1879, and with this play Ibsen aroused a furor among the ranks of the bourgeoisie throughout Europe. Opponents of the femininst movement understood what a powerful influence this play could have among the people, and they denounced the playwright and the woman he had created — Nora was, I think, the first of Ibsen's female characters who was debated and discussed by the public as if she were flesh and blood, a member of the society, instead of a fictional character. In a series of articles published in 1884 in "Luthersk Ugeskrift," pastor M. J. Faerden admonishes his parishioners to beware the new, emancipated woman:

> *Just as Nora appears in the final scene, free and unfettered by any bond, divine or human, without commitment or obligation to the man whom she has given her promise or to the children she has brought into this world — likewise we will find the wife in the modern marriage, from beginning to end. In the future her place will not be in the innermost sanctuary of the home, like a priestess*

at its hearth and altar. The emancipated woman has taken her place at the door, always ready to depart, with her suitcase in her hand. The suitcase — and not, as before, the ring of fidelity — will be the symbol of her role in marriage.[6]

Members of the opposite camp were not slow to voice their opinion, in words equally as passionate. Already in 1880, in the January 12th edition of "Aftenbladet" an article with the heading "The miracle doesn't happen just any old day" was printed. It was signed "G-g," the first and last initials of Gina Krog. (It is interesting to note that the time was still not ripe for women to sign their names to articles and reviews. Amalie Skram, who was just beginning to publish her writings at this time and whom I will discuss later, also signed articles with initials — "ie," the last initials of her first name.) Gina Krog (b. 1847, d. 1916) was a schoolteacher who became a leading figure in the women's movement in Norway, beginning in the 1880s. She was one of the founders of the Norwegian Women's Rights League and was the first editor of "Nylaende," a feminist journal published from 1887 to 1927. In her article on *A Doll's House* Gina Krog observes that for many the book was "like a harbinger of a terrible and destructive storm." But for those of us who have been waiting for these words, she writes, it was "as if the miracle began to happen." She has great faith in the effect Ibsen's words will have on society, that they will cleanse and reform and free women from their doll-like existence. She concludes with heartfelt thanks to the man "to whom we owe this miracle, we cry out our thanks, we can no longer bear this heavy debt of gratitude in silence. We thank for each beautiful vision, we thank because he pronounces judgment on us, so clearly and harshly and without mercy, thank for the fight against falsehood and injustice and for the dawning hope of a springtime that rejuvenates."[7]

A week later, on January 19, Amalie Skram submitted an article on *A Doll's House* to another of Kristiania's newspapers, "Dagbladet." Amalie Skram (b. 1846, d. 1905) is a prominent figure in Norwegian literature who perhaps needs no introduction. Norway's foremost representative of naturalistic literature, Skram is most widely known for the four-volume work, *The People of Hellemyr*, but she also wrote a number of novels in which she probes into the institution of marriage and of the family among members of the bourgeoisie. She is the first Norwegian author to take up the problem of woman's sexuality — her lack of experience, her ignorance, her needs, her desires, her frigidity . . . At the time the article on *A Doll's House* was written, Amalie Skram was not an established writer of fiction. Recently divorced, Amalie Müller, as she was called then, was trying to live from her pen as a literary critic. Her discussions of current literary works are thorough and perceptive, and they reveal her preoccupation with the psychology of the characters and with the external factors determining behavior. Skram praises Ibsen for his success with *A Doll's House*, both as a dramatic masterpiece and as an unparalleled portrayal of human psychology. She discusses all the characters in detail, but in particular her treatment of Nora is exhaustive and insightful. She presents an objective but sympathetic view of this woman who is becoming emancipated. And her conclusion is that Ibsen's play must be regarded and respected as a sign, a warning and a judgment. "When woman awakens to full consciousness of her individual worth, when her eyes have truly been opened to all the injustice that has been committed against her throughout time, then she will arm herself against him, to whom she was given as helper, and she will break all bonds, scale all walls that society and the authority of institutions have built up around her." The judgment, Skram continues, is on marriage which, far from being a union between two people, is an arrangement by which one provides and the other is provided for; with rules that protect the one who provides and reduce his partner to a nonentity.[8]

In her classic study, *The History of the Norwegian Woman's Movement* (published 1937), Anna Caspari Agerholt underlines the tremendous impact *A Doll's House* had on improving the position of women in Scandinavia. "It felt like an attack on conventional marriage, on woman's upbringing and woman's destiny. It was interpreted as a plea for her right to be herself, independent of her task as wife and mother, and for her duty to be a human being, an individual to the same degree as a man."[9] These women Ibsen was bringing to life in the 1870s, 80s, and 90s demanded respect and admiration from women as well as from their male counterparts. Critic Mathilde Schjøtt once remarked that a very upright and religious man had confided to her that Nora's statement "I am a human being" had "lit new lights for him."[10] And it is true that Nora was much more capable of charming society's conservative elements than, say, a Mrs. Alving, or Rebecca West or Hedda Gabler. But if these later women were received with disgust by some, they were hailed with even warmer enthusiasm by the feminists.

The strong-willed and passionate Rebecca West, whose "soiled" past in no way crippled or perverted her moral character and integrity, was welcomed like a breath of sea air. In the magazine "Nylaende" Gina Krog wrote that when she had read *Rosmersholm* it was as if she had heard "proclaimed the gospel of the future" and she reiterated her praise of Ibsen: "Ibsen's belief in women, in the women of his country, has never been expressed so proudly as here."[11]

There had always been discussion as to whom Ibsen's women were modeled after. As I mentioned earlier, it was commonly believed that Aasta Hansteen was the model for Lona Hessel; the dramatic conflict in *A Doll's House* was to a large extent borrowed from an episode in the life of author and friend Laura Kieler, and it is not unlikely that Nora borrowed some of Kieler's characteristics as well; Rebecca West was reportedly greatly inspired by Ibsen's mother-in-law, Magdalene Thoresen, herself a productive writer of short stories and plays; and Camilla Collett was evidently so certain that Ellida Wangel's crisis of the heart was a re-creation of her own unhappy love that she wrote to Ibsen and asked him if this wasn't so. But none of these aforementioned characters gave rise to as much speculation as did Hedda Gabler, by far the most disputed and least understood of Ibsen's women. In an article written in 1893, Mathilde Schjøtt reports that rumor has attributed the honor — or dishonor — of being Hedda Gabler's model to innumerable ladies — Norwegian, Swedish, Danish, German, and English. More recently, in a new full-length study, *Ibsen — The Person and the Artist*, Norwegian professor Daniel Haakonsen points to yet another possible model, the Swedish feminist author Victoria Benedictsson, pseudonym, Ernst Ahlgren.

Victoria Benedictsson was born in 1850, and in 1888 she took her own life. Ibsen had met her briefly in Stockholm in 1886, but he obviously remembered her, because in January 1889 he wrote this to Gustaf af Geijerstam: "Mrs. Benedictsson's death and your sensitive and compassionate depiction of her life have made a lasting impresson on me. I knew her too short a time to truly and deeply understand her that time we met in Stockholm."[12] That same year, 1889, Ellen Key, a leader in the feminist movement in Sweden, published a small book dedicated to the memory of her friend which she titled *Ernst Ahlgren, some biographical notes.* Key brings to light bits and pieces of personal information from Benedictsson's childhood and youth, her unhappy marriage, her periods of illness, her struggle to find time and energy to write, her intimate correspondence with Axel Lundegård, her last years in Copenhagen. As a child she was partial to her father, an outdoorsman whose dream to pursue a career in the military had not been realized. In Benedictsson's own words: "He taught me to ride, to wrestle, to shoot with a pistol as well as other manly sports; he treated me quite like a boy."[13] Many years later, in 1884, she entered into an intimate relationship with another man, a young, rebellious writer named Axel Lundegård. For two years they kept up an active correspondence in which they address each other as Comrade! and discuss literature and philosophy, the need to be honest and true to one's own self, as well as topics which, in that time of Victorian morality, were taboo for women. These and other letters Key had at her disposal reveal a number of interesting things about Victoria Benedictsson: Not only did Benedictsson know and admire Ibsen's works, she literally echoed some of his most cherished ideas — the longing for freedom, the demand that the individual pursue self-realization, the belief that work can give life real meaning, a desire to surround herself with beauty. Is it not tempting to imagine that Ibsen read this book that came out just one year before his own *Hedda Gabler*?

I find it rather curious that at the same time there are so many "live" models for this character, one also hears the accusation that Hedda Gabler is exaggerated and not a realistic figure — real women simply don't act like Hedda Gabler! An essay bearing the title "Has Henrik Ibsen portrayed real women in *Hedda Gabler*?" appeared in Kristiania in 1891. The author was simply "A woman's voice," an early pseudonym for Hanna Andresen Butenschøn. (She later published five novels, three plays, and her memoirs under the pseudonym Helene Dickmar.) It is remarkable that this study has been overlooked and forgotten by later Ibsen scholars, for it greatly impressed and pleased the poet himself, as well as other critics of the day. Ibsen wrote a letter to Mrs. Butenschøn thanking her for her essay: "Your interpretation of my work is sensitive and perceptive in every respect. You have overlooked nothing nor have you added anything from your own imagination. And for this I am deeply appreciative."[14] I regret that I do not have the time now to give this study anything but brief mention. Her answer is, of course, that Hedda is a real woman, and she explains this dark and mysterious female with these words:

> *A woman whose deepest female instincts have been disturbed and distorted due in part to faults of her own, in part to cruel fate; and who ends up breathing in an atmosphere where all her peculiar shortcomings sprout like gigantic, foul smelling and poisonous flowers, which ultimately kill her.*[15]

The relationship between these feminist authors and critics and Ibsen's women characters is reciprocal: It was the feminists of the 1870s and 80s who gave their heartblood to the creation of Nora, Rebecca West, Hedda Gabler, but this initial inspiration was matched and returned tenfold. In fact, we are still collecting in 1982. As a conclusion to my discussion I will read an excerpt from an article by Mathilde Schjøtt, written in response to N. Hertzberg's brochure, "Are Ibsen's Women Characters Norwegian?" Mr. Hertzberg laments the fact that Ibsen is no longer creating "ideal" women as he did in his early plays, and Schjøtt responds by asking if "this womanliness is not an expression for how man *dreams* about woman in his youth, and beyond this, an expression for how he later finds it most comfortable that she should be." Having observed this, and having determined that he shall depict life as it is, Schjøtt argues, must not the poet (namely Ibsen) renounce that kind of womanliness "not solely in the name of cold reality, but also in the name of human dignity, of men and of women. In other words, does not this change represent moral progress? For it can scarcely be considered moral or dignified for a man to be like Peer Gynt, whole and true only in a woman's belief, hope and love, and to not bear the responsibility for his own life. It is not until men witness the moral irresponsibility of women such as Nora, Rebecca West, Hedda Gabler, that they are horrified at what their immorality has brought about."[16]

NOTES

[1]Anna Caspari Agerholt, *Den norske kvinnebevegelses historie*, new edition ed. Kari Skjønsberg, (Gyldendal: Oslo 1973), p. 33.

[2]*Mannssamfunnet midt imot. Norsk kvinnesaksdebatt gjennom tre mannsalder*, ed. Kari Skjønsberg, (Gyldendal: Oslo 1974), pp. 33-34.

[3]*The Correspondence of Henrik Ibsen*, trans. & ed. Mary Morison, (Haskell House Publisher Ltd.: New York 1970), p. 365.

[4]*Ibid.*, pp. 423-24.

[5]*Gjennom kvinneøyne. Norske kvinners litteraturkritikk og reaksjon på litteratur ca 1880-1930*, ed. Åse Hiorth Lervik, (Universitetsforlaget: Oslo 1980), p. 21.

[6]Agerholt, p. 37.

[7]*Ibid.*, p. 37.

[8]Amalie Skram, "En Betragtning over "Et Dukkehjem," ("Dagbladet:" January 19, 1880), pp. 2-3.

[9]Agerholt, p. 36.

[10]*Mannssamfunnet midt imot*, p. 64. (This quote appeared in an article by Mathilde Schjøtt, "Om kvinners stilling og adgang til høyere utdannelse" printed in "Vor Ungdom" 1884.)

[11]Agerholt, p. 38.

[12]*Correspondence of Henrik Ibsen*, p. 334.

[13]Ellen Key, *Ernst Ahlgren. Några Biografiske Meddelanden*, (Z. Haeggströms Förlagsexpedition: Stockholm 1889), p. 9

[14]*Henrik Ibsen Brev 1845-1905, Ny Samling*, ed. Øyvind Anker, (Universitetsforlaget: Oslo 1979), p. 375.

[15]Elisabeth Ebbing, "Hedda Gabler, En kvinderøst og Henrik Ibsen," *Edda 6* (1978), pp. 341-343.

[16]*Gjennom kvinneøyne*, p. 97.

Charles S. Gilpin as the Emporer Jones.

Charles Gilpin: Opening the Way for the American Black Actor

Laurilyn J. Harris

When George Cram Cook first heard Eugene O'Neill read his new play, *The Emperor Jones*, he told Susan Glaspell that "the Emperor has got to be a black man. A blacked-up white is not in the spirit of this production."[1] Therefore, Cook, who directed the first production of *The Emperor Jones* for the Provincetown Players in 1920, cast an experienced black actor, Charles Gilpin, in the role of Brutus Jones. Cook's judgment proved sound, for Gilpin's performance "scored a success that provided one of the major theatrical sensations of the season."[2] The critical acclaim that Gilpin received for his skillful execution of a difficult role marked the high point of a long and arduous acting career, but the consequences of his success reached beyond the limits of a personal triumph. Because of his work in *The Emperor Jones*, "Gilpin reached the highest point of achievement on the legitimate stage that had yet been attained by a Negro in America,"[3] and thereby did much to shatter the illusion that black actors were fit only for vaudeville and minstrel shows. By choosing a Black to play a leading role in a significant American drama, the Provincetown Players provided "the initial and greatest force in opening up the way for the Negro on the dramatic stage."[4] Gilpin became known as the "torchbearer"[5], the symbol of the progress of the American black actor in achieving recognition as a serious dramatic artist.

Despite his initial decision to cast a Black in the title role, Cook had misgivings when the time came to choose his actors. After all, no Negro had ever played a major role in an American tragedy before.[6] The great dramatic actor Ira Aldridge had performed Shakespearean roles in the 1860's, but his success had been restricted to England and Germany.[7] In America, Blacks were for the most part confined by tradition to minstrel shows ("a caricature of Negro life"[8]), musical playlets such as *A Trip to Coontown* (1898), and minor roles in Broadway shows. Entertainers such as comedian Bert Williams and singer Sissieretta Jones enjoyed great popularity with both Negro and white audiences, but their home was the vaudeville circuit. Black companies — the Pekin Players in Chicago and the Lafayette Players in Harlem — presented serious drama to black audiences, but attracted little notice from the critics or the general public. Therefore, it is not surprising that Cook was slightly wary of casting a Black, for minstrelsy and vaudeville had fixed the image of the Negro in the public mind as "an irresponsible, happy-go-lucky, wide-grinning, loud-laughing, shuffling, banjo-playing . . . sort of being."[9] Cook thought that perhaps a white actor such as Charles Ellis could play

Laurilyn J. Harris is Chairperson of the Department of Speech at Washington State University.

the role in black-face, but auditions soon reinforced his earlier opinion that only a Black could successfully portray the character of the Emperor. Burns Mantle recorded that "when they came to cast *The Emperor Jones* the Provincetown folk discovered that none of the white actors who were given a chance at it could read convincingly the speeches given to Brutus Jones. They therefore determined to try a negro player in the role."[10] Jasper Deeter, who had been cast as Smithers, had seen Gilpin play the role of Custis, a Negro minister, in Drinkwater's *Abraham Lincoln* in 1919. Cook, impressed by Deeter's report of Gilpin's performance, went to Harlem to find him. According to one report, Cook found him running an elevator.[11] Other sources seem equally convinced that Gilpin was then employed as a ticket-clipper on the Sixth Avenue el.[12] In any case, Cook persuaded him to come to the tiny Provincetown Playhouse on Macdougal Street and read for the part. According to Susan Glaspell, he was cast after one reading: "When he [Cook] heard that voice on those lines — 'It's a go,' said Jig to Gilpin."[13]

Thus Charles Gilpin became the first professional actor to perform at the Provincetown, [14] and Cook could not have chosen an actor with wider or more varied theatrical experience. Gilpin was born in 1878 in Richmond, Virginia, "where he had felt the sting of race prejudice and become embittered by it."[15] At the age of twelve, he decided to supplement his salary as a printer's devil by forming a quartet with three other black youngsters to sing in restaurants in the evenings. Then he naturally gravitated into show business. He travelled with small road shows and vaudeville acts ("had been stranded more than once"[16]), and was a member of a minstrel troupe, a street fair, a concert company, a group of jubilee singers, and William and Walker's Cake-Walk Company. In between theatrical jobs, he stayed alive by working as a barber, printer, janitor, elevator-boy, switchboard operator, and, like Brutus Jones, a Pullman porter. From 1907 to 1909, he worked with the Pekin Stock Company, thereby gaining experience in playing legitimate drama. After the company disbanded, he went to New York, and worked in the two best Black theatres in Harlem: the Anita Bush Players at the Lincoln Theatre, and the Lafayette Players at the Lafayette Theatre. He himself helped to organize the Lafayette Players, who presented comedies, tragedies, and melodramas, and he managed the group in 1916.[17] He was discovered at the Lafayette in 1919 by Lester Lonergan, who was producing *Abraham Lincoln*. The role which Lonergan offered Gilpin was that of Custis, an old Negro minister with a "preposterous American Indian dialect."[18] Gilpin was at first reluctant to accept the role, because "he felt that he was too old and the bitterness of disappointment in addition to the possible loss of his job as an elevator boy"[19] made him cautious in taking a role in a Broadway show. He played the part, however, and attracted favorable notice: "the conference between the President and the black man constituting one of the strongest and most touching scenes in the play."[20] After the run was over, he returned to the Lafayette Players and his elevator. Cook later said "here is a man who for years has had it in him to mount to the top of the ladder, and there was no ladder on which a man of his race could set foot."[21]

The Provincetown Players were happy to provide the first step on that ladder. Even from the initial rehearsals, it became apparent that "he and the Emperor Jones were a classic example of actor and part meeting to perfection."[22] The role is extremely difficult — *The Emperor Jones* is a one-man show, a "monologue of terror"[23] which rises to a pitch of almost unbearable emotional intensity. Six of the eight scenes are entirely monologue, and "the sheer physical feat of sustaining the part . . . demanded admiration."[24] But the character of Brutus Jones demands more than physical stamina from an actor. O'Neill's play reveals through the disintegration of the Emperor's personality "the progressive steps in a study of personal and racial psychology of real imaginative truth."[25] Indeed, the success of the play depends upon the leading actor's ability to project the emotionally complex picture of "a human soul fighting against his own evil deeds, the cruel fate of his forefathers, the ignorance of centuries."[26] However, "the author was fortunate in the acting of Mr. Gilpin,"[27] for he possessed not only the physical and emotional power needed to sustain the role, but also the technical skills, gained by years of stage experience, to use those powers with the utmost effect. Physically, Gilpin was well-suited to play the Emperor, who is described in the script as "a tall, powerfully-built, full-blooded negro of middle age."[28] Gilpin was forty-two years old, "handsome, light-skinned, brawny,"[29] and had "a pair of somber eyes, which seemed to be burned into his face."[30] The force of the emotions he projected on stage was overwhelming. Cook, after watching him at a rehearsal, remarked that "when we watch Gilpin in this play, we do not stop at feeling what a negro in these circumstances feels and does and says: we are made partakers of the experience of a man in the grip of terror."[31] Moss Hart, seeing Gilpin rehearse for a later revival of the play, was likewise awed by the impact of his performance: "the effect was shattering. He had an inner violence and a maniacal power that engulfed the spectator."[32] O'Neill was indeed fortunate to find in Gilpin an actor so well-suited to perform the most significant role in his new play. In fact, at least one critic of the day asserted that "his magnificent interpretation of that part has had much to do with the sudden rise to fame of Eugene O'Neill."[33]

The Emperor Jones opened at the Provincetown Playhouse on November 1, 1920, and "The next morning Gilpin was famous."[34] His acting was enthusiastically acclaimed by both the critics and the public. Heywood Broun, critic for the *Tribune,* stated:

> *The Emperor is played by a negro actor named Charles S. Gilpin, who gives the most thrilling performance we have seen any place this season. . . . He sustains the succession of scenes in monologue not only because his voice is one of a gorgeous natural quality, but because he knows just what to do with it. All the notes are there and he has also an extraordinary facility for being in the right place at the right time.*[35]

S. Jay Kaufman, critic for the *Dramatic Mirror,* wrote that "the finest performance in years is undoubtedly Charles Gilpin's."[36] Alexander Woollcott reviewed *The Emperor Jones* for the *Times*, and although he thought the play was "clumsily produced,"[37] he had nothing but praise for Gilpin:

> *It weaves a most potent spell, thanks partly to the force and cunning of its author, thanks partly to the admirable playing of Charles S. Gilpin in a title role so predominant that the play is little more than a dramatic monologue. His is an uncommonly powerful and imaginative performance, in several respects unsurpassed this season in New York. Mr. Gilpin is a Negro. . . . They [Provincetown Players] have acquired an actor, one who has it in him to invoke the pity and the terror and the indescribable foreboding which are part of the secret of* The Emperor Jones.[38]

The most complete review of Gilpin's performance was given by Kenneth Macgowan, reviewer for the *Globe*, who later expanded his review for *Theatre Arts Magazine*:

> *To the skill of its producers and the lesson of the sky-dome, the Provincetown Players have added in this production a magnificent piece of acting. From Harlem they brought a colored player, Charles Gilpin, to impersonate the emperor. . . . In* The Emperor Jones *he shows not only a great power and a great imagination, in addition to his fine voice, but he displays an extraordinary versatility. It is a genuine impersonation, a being of flesh and blood and brain utterly different from the actor's other work. He carries the long soliloquy of the six scenes in the forest with extraordinary ease, building up steadily from his fright at the first Little Formless Fears, through his terror at the recurring visions of his crimes, to the horror that overwhelms him as the dim, buried, racial fears rise to carry him back to the auction block, the slave ship, and the voodoo gods of the Congo. Mr. Gilpin's performance is the crown to a play that opens up the imagination of the American Theatre, and builds beauty and emotion out of the spiritual realities of one corner of our life.*[39]

Macgowan considered Gilpin's performance "a sustained and splendid piece of acting,"[40] and added that "the moment when he raises his naked body against the moonlit sky beyond the edge of the jungle and prays, is such a dark lyric of the flesh, such a cry of the primitive being, as I have never seen in the theatre."[41]

To their amazement, the Provincetown Players found themselves with an instant hit. Since their semi-professional theatre was open to subscribers only, a thousand new members were enrolled the first week of the run.[42] The tiny theatre seated only 150 persons, and old subscribers who arrived the second night of performance to claim their seats "could not get near the box office."[43] The original engagement of two weeks was extended again and again, until Adolph Klauber persuaded the Players to transfer the play to a larger theatre uptown on Broadway.[44] *The Emperor Jones* opened at the Selwyn Theatre on December 27, and played for five weeks. Crowded houses forced them to move to a still larger theatre, the Princess, on January 29, where the show played 204 performances before closing the week of May 14, still playing to capacity crowds[45], to begin a two-year road tour.

The success of *The Emperor Jones* brought Gilpin immediate fame as a great dramatic artist, since his fortunes were inextricably bound up with those of the play. Several newspapers, including the *Times*, maintained that not only was Gilpin's acting superb, but also that "the success of the O'Neill play is dependent on it."[46] Burns Mantle recorded that "within a comparatively short time the town was buzzing with its discovery of him as a really 'great actor'."[47] Honors were heaped upon him. In 1920, segments of *The Emperor Jones* were transmitted over radio with Gilpin in the title role — "the first serious drama to be broadcast 'in the history of the radio wireless'."[48] Gilpin received the Spingarn Medal, an award granted annually since 1914 by the National Association for the Advancement of Colored People for "the highest or noblest achievement by an American Negro during the preceding year or years."[49] The Drama League voted him one of the ten persons who had done the most for the American theatre during the year.[50] He was invited to speak at meetings such as that of the New York Theatre Club at the Hotel Astor in 1921, and his appearances at such functions were recorded in newspaper social columns.[51]

Ironically, Gilpin seemed to be the only person aware that his new stature might be short-lived. He knew only too well that he had previously been tied by his dark skin to a chance role now and then, and that, once the run of *The Emperor Jones* was finished, he might find himself running an elevator again. He stated:

> *I am pleased, especially with the generous praise of the critics. But I don't fool myself about the stone walls that are in my way. Mr. O'Neill made a breach in those walls by writing a play that had in it a serious role for a Negro. The Provincetown Players gave me the chance to do the part. But — what next? If I were white, a dozen opportunities would come to me as a result of a success like this. But I'm black. It is no joke when I ask myself, 'Where do I go from here?' Whatever happens, I shall have some evidence to prove that I was not a fool in thinking that a Negro can act. . . . It has been demonstrated that a play can be written that will give a colored actor a chance. Perhaps someone will write another such play. Anyway, if I can't get anything else to play, I suppose I can at least 'play the game.' After all, that's what everyone has to do, one way or another.*[52]

In an address to the Civic Club on "The Negro and the American Stage" in March, 1921, he pleaded for better opportunities for the black actor on the American stage, and asserted that many fine black actors would be developed if they could act in legitimate drama — "there is no reason," he said, "why we should do nothing but buffoonery."[53]

One aspect of the "stone wall" which Gilpin and all black actors faced was demonstrated by the reaction to Gilpin's Drama League award as one of the ten outstanding theatrical figures of 1920. It was the custom for the recipients of this award to attend the annual Drama League banquet in March as honored guests.[54] Certain members of the League suddenly realized that they would be dining with a "colored" person, and "wrote to the officers of the League protesting against the seating of a negro at table with his white brothers and sisters."[55] The League withdrew its invitation to Gilpin on the flimsy excuse that "his acting, although distinctive, had shown his own race to bad advantage, and therefore was not in his favor."[56] The press quickly picked up the story, and "thereupon broke out a controversy that divided the Drama League, the theatrical profession, the press, and the public."[57] Eugene O'Neill, one of the other "honored guests", was infuriated at the insult to his star — especially since he himself was invited for writing *The Emperor Jones*. O'Neill and Macgowan paid calls on the other actors who were invited, urging them to decline their invitations.[58] Many actors complied with their request, and the combination of the sudden influx of refusals to attend and the sensational publicity the story was receiving from the press (most of it unfavorable to the League[59]) caused the League to re-issue its invitation to Gilpin. The dinner was a great success, with 1,000 guests attending as compared with the previous year's 300. When Macgowan, as toastmaster, introduced Gilpin as "the greatest actor of his race,"[60] the audience responded with "tremendous applause."[61] Nevertheless, the incident must have heightened Gilpin's awareness that prejudice was still a formidable barrier to the black actor.

Gilpin's first-hand experience with prejudice, even at the height of his fame, plus his awareness that an opportunity to play a role such as Brutus Jones might never again come his way, served to embitter him despite the days of success and applause. To shut out the reality of what lay beyond the run of *The Emperor Jones*, he turned to the bottle. Moss Hart observed that:

> *He was limited not by his own range as an actor, but by the limitations of the part the Negro could play in the theatre. Had he not been a Negro, there is no doubt that he would have been one of the great actors of his time, but other than the Emperor Jones, there were no parts of any stature that ever came his way. Not unnaturally, his success in* The Emperor Jones *and the probability that he would never play anything else worthy of his talent, embittered an already violent and hostile nature, and he took what refuge and solace he could find in alcohol.*[62]

Under the influence of his drinking, his performance began gradually to deteriorate: "he became undependable, behavior erratic, at times drinking too much to give an effective performance."[63] O'Neill, annoyed, began to complain, especially when Gilpin, "who had grown suddenly finicky about using the word 'nigger' (called for by the script), was rewriting the role . . . substituting 'black baby' and other terms he considered more genteel."[64] O'Neill, who had an intense phobia against "goddam hams"[65] who rewrote his lines or grew sloppy in performance during a run, was furious. After one performance where Gilpin had taken liberties with the script, O'Neill rushed backstage screaming "if I ever catch you rewriting my lines again, you black bastard, I'm going to beat you up."[66] When the road tour ended in 1923, and plans were being discussed for a European tour, O'Neill decided that he had had enough of Gilpin. Believing that "Gilpin lived under the assumption that no one could be got to play his part and took advantage accordingly,"[67] O'Neill grimly set out to find a replacement for him. He discovered an ex-law student named Paul Robeson, and triumphantly proclaimed:

> *Gilpin is all 'Ham' and a yard wide! . . . He was drunk all of last season. . . . So I've corralled a young fellow with considerable experience, wonderful presence and voice, and . . . real brains — not a 'ham'. . . . I'm sure he'll be bigger than Gilpin was even at the start.*[68]

Therefore, Gilpin was not asked to play Brutus Jones in the Provincetown revivals of the play in May, 1924 and December, 1925, nor in the London production in the summer of 1925. But although Robeson was a brilliant successor to Gilpin, Gilpin was "heartbroken"[69] when he realized that the part he had considered his personal property had been given to another. After seeing Robeson play the role in 1925, he sadly remarked, "I feel kind of low. I created the role of the Emperor. That role belongs to me. That Irishman, he just wrote the play."[70]

After 1923, Gilpin's career went steadily downhill. Because of the unavailability of good roles for Blacks, he was limited to parts in minor plays such as the 1924 revival of Nan Stephen's folk play *Roseanne,* in which he played the Reverend Brown, and countless revivals of *The Emperor Jones* (he played the role over 1,000 times[71]) by groups other than the Provincetown Players. Moss Hart played Smithers to his Jones in a revival at the Mayfair Theatre in 1925, and asserted that Gilpin, when sober, still possessed much of his old power in the role: "at his best, which he was that night [opening] and not very often afterward, he was a spectacular and memorable Emperor Jones. Even on the wrong side of the proscenium . . . I was caught up and held by the majesty and grandeur of his performance."[72] Unfortunately, by 1925, he was playing far more performances drunk than sober, and the result was often painfully ludicrous. Hart described one such performance:

> *Mr. Gilpin was a little less than sober that evening and . . . the management had decided that rather than refund the money they would get him into his costume, push him out on the stage, and take a chance on what would happen. . . . Gilpin made his entrance stumblingly, quite as though he had been pushed out from the wings — which indeed he was — and made directly for the throne, where he sat down heavily and proceeded to go to sleep. . . . I pulled him to his feet, and hanging onto his arm to steady him, I yelled my first line into his ear. Astonishingly, he answered with the correct line. . . . Haltingly Gilpin began to play. His voice*

> *was thick, and he jumbled the cues, but he sat on the throne steadying himself until he regained something like control over his movements, and then he rose and as the act proceeded he even seemed to play with something of his old power.*[73]

Aside from the revivals, Gilpin never played another major role in New York. Finally, broken by drink and ill-health, he retired to a small farm in New Jersey, where he died in 1930 at the age of fifty-one. A eulogy in the *Herald Tribune* included the significant comment that "one of America's great actors is dead, and he will be remembered for a single role."[74]

A single role — a sad waste for a talented actor such as Gilpin, who, given the opportunity, could perhaps have created many fine roles. Ironically, his success in *The Emperor Jones* helped to destroy him, for he realized, even when his popularity was at its height, that the road he had opened for others lay closed to him. He was too broken and too embittered to benefit from the new interest of playwrights such as O'Neill and Torrence in using the Negro and Negro life as pure dramatic material, or to attempt Shakespearean roles such as Othello. But Gilpin, by proving to the critics that the black actor could perform effectively in legitimate drama, opened the way for the progress of younger actors such as Robeson. "Another important page in the history of the Negro in the theatre was written,"[75] for the image of the shuffling, good natured Negro of the minstrel shows was shattered. Indeed, by 1924, a number of eminent critics enthusiastically proclaimed that Blacks in theatre were potentially better actors than their white counterparts. For example, George Nathan wrote that "the black man is far better fitted naturally for the profession of acting than his white brother . . . the Negro is a born actor, where the white man achieves acting."[76] While in the modern context such statements sound somewhat derogatory (the "all-blacks-got-rhythm" syndrome) at least the potential of blacks as theatre artists was at last being recognized.

Although Gilpin performed only one major role on Broadway, he not only won serious critical attention for future black actors, but also seems to have awakened the interest of playwrights in racial themes which provided black actors with substantial roles (*All God's Chillun Got Wings, Lost in the Stars,* etc.). His fine interpretation of Brutus Jones helped to establish the growing reputation of Eugene O'Neill, and "the portrait of the Emperor is still recognized as Gilpin's contribution to the American theatre almost as much as it is O'Neill's."[77] Perhaps his greatest tribute came from the playwright who once threatened to beat him up. In 1946, O'Neill, looking back over three decades of experience with actors, stated that "I can honestly say there was only one actor who carried out every notion of a character I had in mind. That actor was Charles Gilpin as the Pullman porter in *The Emperor Jones.*"[78]

NOTES

[1]Susan Glaspell, *The Road to the Temple* (New York: Frederick A. Stokes Co., 1927), p. 287.

[2]Burns Mantle, ed., *The Best Plays of 1920-21* (Boston: Small, Maynard & Company, 1921), p. 6.

[3]James Weldon Johnson, *Black Manhattan* (New York: Alfred A. Knopf, 1930), pp. 184-5.

[4]Helen Deutsch and Stella Hanau, *The Provincetown, a Story of the Theatre* (New York: Farrar & Rinehart, Inc., 1931), p. 71.

[5]Benjamin Brawley, *The Negro Genius* (New York: Dodd, Mead, & Co., 1937), p. 289.

[6]Arthur and Barbara Gelb, *O'Neill* (New York: Harper & Brothers, 1960), p. 445.

[7]See Herbert Marshall and Mildred Stock, *Ira Aldridge: The Negro Tragedian* (Carbondale: Southern Illinois University Press, 1968).

[8]Johnson, p. 93.

[9]Ibid.

[10]Mantle, p. 299.

[11]Oliver M. Sayler, *Our American Theatre* (New York: Brentano's, 1923), p. 98.

[12]Gelb, p. 445.

[13]Glaspell, p. 289.

[14]Deutsch and Hanau, pp. 63-64.

[15]Gelb, p. 445.

[16]Johnson, p. 185.

[17]Phyllis Hartnoll, ed., *The Oxford Companion to the Theatre, 2nd ed., (London: Oxford University Press, 1957), p. 321.*

[18]*Deutsch and Hanau, p. 64.*

[19]*Robert T. Holland, "The American Negro Theatre: A Development of and Reaction Against the Minstrel Concept" (Master's thesis, State University of Iowa, 1944), p. 102.*

[20]*Johnson, p. 182.*

[21]*Glaspell, p. 289.*

[22]*Moss Hart, Act One* (New York: Random House, 1959), p. 98.

[23]Gelb, p. 440.

[24]Johnson, p. 184.

[25]Kenneth Macgowan, "The New Season," *Theatre Arts Magazine*, 5 (January 1921): 6.

[26]Arthur Hobson Quinn, *A History of the American Drama*, 2 vols. (New York; F. S. Crofts & Co., 1936), 2: 179.

[27]Jack Crawford, "Broadway in Mid-Career," *The Drama*, 2 (January 1921): 138.

[28]Eugene O'Neill, *The Emperor Jones*, in *Nine Plays by Eugene O'Neill* (New York: The Modern Library, 1959), p. 5.

[29]Gelb, p. 445.

[30]Hart, p. 98.

[31]Glaspell, p. 289.

[32]Hart, p. 98.

[33]*New York Herald Tribune*, 10 May 1937, as quoted in Holland, p. 105.

[34]Johnson, p. 184.

[35]As quoted in Brawley, p. 289.

[36]S. J. Kaufman, "Resume of the Season?," *Dramatic Mirror and Theatre World*, 83 (May 14, 1921): 805.

[37]*New York Times*, 7 November 1920, Section 2, p. 1.

[38]Ibid.

[39]Macgowan: 6-7.

[40]As quoted in Deutsch and Hanau, p. 67.

[41]Ibid.

[42]Ibid., p. 68.

[43]Ibid., p. 63

[44]Ibid., p. 71.

[45]*Dramatic Mirror* (May 14, 1921): 817.

[46]*New York Times*, as quoted in Holland, p. 103.

[47]Mantle, p. 6.

[48]Gelb, p. 720.

[49]Johnson, p. 185.

[50]Ibid., p. 184.

[51]*Dramatic Mirror*, 83 (February 12, 1921): 282.
[52]As quoted in Gelb, p. 448.
[53]As quoted in the *Dramatic Mirror*, 83 (March 12, 1921): 442.
[54]Gelb, p. 448.
[55]Mantle, p. 6.
[56]*Dramatic Mirror*, 83 (February 19, 1921): 323.
[57]Johnson, p. 185.
[58]Gelb, p. 448.
[59]*Dramatic Mirror*, 83 (February 26, 1921): 362.
[60]Ibid., (March 12, 1921): 442.
[61]Ibid.
[62]Hart, pp. 98-99.
[63]Gelb, p. 449.
[64]Ibid.
[65]As quoted in Ibid., p. 424.
[66]As quoted in Ibid., p. 424.
[67]Ibid., p. 450.
[68]Ibid., 449-450.
[69]Ibid., p. 450.
[70]As quoted in Ibid.
[71]Hart, p. 98.
[72]Ibid., p. 101.
[73]Ibid., pp. 102-103.
[74]*New York Herald Tribune*, 10 May 1930, as quoted in Holland, p. 105.
[75]Johnson, pp. 183-184.
[76]As quoted in Eslanda Robeson, *Paul Robeson, Negro* (New York: Harper & Brothers, 1930), p. 82.
[77]Edith J. Isaacs, *The Negro in the American Theatre (New York: Theatre Arts, Inc., 1947), p. 63.*
[78]*As quoted in Gelb, p. 448.*

The Popular Response to Tommaso Salvini in America

David H. Fennema

Tommaso Salvini, who established his reputation in North America during the 1880's, has all but disappeared in the annals of American theatre history. This actor, who appeared on the stages of France, South America, the United States, England, Egypt, Russia, Austria, Germany and, in his homeland, Italy, survives mainly in articles and reviews hidden in library archives. Many of his still famous and recognized contemporaries — Edwin Booth, Joseph Jefferson III, Henry Irving, Sarah Bernhardt, Stanislavski — all make reference to Salvini in their autobiographies, and numerous articles by him and about him appeared in periodicals during his life-time. Yet, with this great record of his life and achievements available, few scholars of theatre history have taken the time to explore Salvini.

During Salvini's fifth and final tour of the United States, his friend, John Ward Dunsmore, was quoted in an interview published by the *Detroit Free Press* (5 January 1890, p. 6, col. 1):

> *[Salvini] is gravely impressed with the fact that his art cannot be perpetuated after him, but must die when he is called away. To Salvini this is a thought of deep sadness. . . . [T]he words of the actor die with the hour, and if they live at all, exist only as a memory. Such was the fate of Forrest and Kean. Such will be the fate of Salvini. It is indeed a sad yet unavailing truth that an actor is only for his generation. After he is gone, to write that he was the best of his time means little or nothing.*

Because of his strong pride in being an Italian, his attitudes towards publicity and his conservative life-style, Salvini is little known today. Examining Salvini's popular reception in America, with emphasis on his first American tour in 1873-74, will help focus attention on his significance in American theatre history.

It was during the summer of 1871 that Salvini was first contacted by Maurice Grau regarding a tour of North America. Jacob Grau, Maurice's uncle, had started negotiating with Salvini at the end of his South American tour (1870-1871), but due to a sudden illness which resulted in Jacob's death, a contract was never signed. Salvini was at first very reluctant to consider an American tour and was filled with doubt. South America had been easy to "conquer" because of its close affinities in language and culture; such was not the case with North America. The only Italian who had attempted such a venture was Ristori and her success had been marginal. Salvini

David H. Fennema is Assistant Professor in the Department of Theatre at the University of Denver.

pondered the idea several months before reaching the decision to undertake the venture. The fact that both of Ristori's American tours (1866 and 1867) had been managed by Jacob Grau, plus Ristori's friendship with Salvini certainly influenced his decision.

Salvini's name was not unknown in the United States in the 1870's. Between 1859 and 1863, William W. Story's book, *Roba Di Roma,* which was serialized in the *Atlantic Monthly* prior to its publication in book form, had introduced the Italian actor to American readers. While in Italy, Story met Robert and Elizabeth Browning, with whom he became close friends. The Brownings showed their excitement over Salvini's performances in their letters of 1859:

> *Salvini is playing every night but in his stupid little French* comediettes. *When he begins his great performances, I shall go. (7 January 1859, Robert Browning to Isabella Blagden).*[1]

> *. . . we have been caught and sent several times to the theatre (so unusual for us) to see the great actor, Salvini, who is about to leave Florence. We saw him in 'Othello' and in 'Hamlet' and he was very great in both, Robert thought, as well as I. Only his houses pine, because, as he says, the 'true tragedies spoil the false,' and the Italians have given up the theatres for the cafes at this moment of crisis. . . . (June, 1859, Elizabeth Browning to Sarianna Browning).*[2]

Story obviously saw Salvini act and was as impressed as the Brownings. Story's *Roba Di Roma* contained the first review of Salvini's acting in English.

> *Salvini, who is of the same school of acting as Modena, has almost an equal genius. His Saul is a wonderful performance, worthy to stand beside the Louis XI of Modena. So, too, his Othello, in another way, is quite as remarkable. The tragedy moved on with an even and constantly accelerating pace from beginning to end. The quiet dignity of the first scenes, where he shows the gentle manliness of his love, and pleads his cause — the turbulent changes of passion when, stung by the poisonous insinuations of lago, he tortures himself by doubts, and writhes at last in the toils of jealousy and madness — the plaintive sorrow and pathos of his suffering — the fierce savageness of his attack on lago, when, in a moment of revulsion, he seizes him by the throat, and flinging him to the ground, towers over him in a tempest of frightful rage — his cruel, bitter taunting of Desdemona, when, wrought upon by lago, he believes her guilty — and the last fearful scene before the murder, where he bids her confess her sins and pray, are given with a gradation and power, compared with which all English representations seem cold and artificial. Nothing is European in his embodiment of Othello; it is the inflammatory passion of the east bursting forth like fire, and consuming a noble and tortured nature — it is the Moor himself as Shakespeare drew him.*

[The review continues with detailed descriptions of how Salvini plays the deaths of Desdemona and Othello.][3]

This passage was often quoted in Salvini's publicity prior to his first American appearance.

Story's home in the Palazzo Barberini was often visited by international travelers and Salvini was one of them. "The sculptor [Story] converted one large room into a theatre with footlights where he presented plays, sometimes written by himself, and in one of these he acted with his friend Salvini who was so famous later as Iago and Othello. Salvini was just entering on the renowned career in which he made Anglo-Saxon actors seem cold and artificial."[4]

Thus, in 1873, Salvini was about to tour an unknown country playing in a language foreign to his audiences. He was filled with uncertainties and doubts, but his friendship with the Storys gave him the assurance that he would know some Americans in Boston and New York. He was also greatly induced by the financial gains of the South American tour and by his contract with Grau which seemed both very good and very encouraging in all ways. He was about to begin the first of what would become five tours of the United States.

On 10 September, 1873, Tommaso Salvini landed in New York. The following day, his arrival was announced by the *New York Times* (11 September 1873, p. 4, col. 6):

> *Signor Tommaso Salvini, the distinguished Italian tragedian, . . . arrived by the Europe last evening. As night had closed in when the vessel reached the Lower Bay, she cast anchor at 7 o'clock, the officers intending to land the passengers this morning. An agreeable surprise, however, was in reserve for Signor Salvini, for, half an hour later, the tug William Fletcher, with a party of the tragedian's admirers aboard, steamed up and welcomed him to America.*

This group of "admirers" was from the Italian colony in New York and had the tug fly the Italian tri-colors in honor of Salvini.[5]

Part of this group of well-wishers included the American press. In his autobiography Salvini recorded his reactions to the reporters and to his initial reception:

> *. . . and it is not enough to say that the reporters did their best in order to have notices of the voyage, of the welcome, of my impressions of the crossing, in the newspapers. Descending on land, and in a carriage, accompanied by my Manager [Maurice Grau], I went to the Everett-House: a comfortable inn, but where the prices pay more than comfort. New people came to find me, and by repeated interrogations and by continual conversations, they made my head like a balloon, ...*[6]

Celso Salvini, in his untranslated biography, added:

> *As soon as he disembarks in New York . . . he is assaulted — of course — by a regiment of reporters. For as much as he knows by hear-say of the customs and tyrannies of the American publicity people, the reality with which he is confronted surpasses all imaginations. He would like to put everybody at the door, because he wants to rest a bit at the hotel . . . but Grau exhorts him to have patience: the 'interviews' are an obligation, . . . and it would be very discourteous not to want to print them.*[7]

Salvini's desire for peace and privacy initially added to his artistic mystique; but, eventually, helped to isolate him from his American admirers.

During the next five days, Salvini rehearsed, toured the city of New York and attended social gatherings in his honor. His first impressions of America were:

> *Whether it was the benefit of a finer air, moved, oxygenated; or the conveniences of material life; whether it was admiration for that busy, industrious, work-loving people, or the beautiful women that by the thousands were met on the street, elegantly dressed, with free and dignified carriage, with a wholesome and lively aspect, or whether it was the thought that these citizens were the great-grandchildren of those noble ones who had known how to win with their blood the independence of their county, I felt as if I was reborn to a new existence, my lungs opened more freely, breathing that air filled with so much life, so much motion, so much freedom and it seemed to be that I had returned to age twenty passing through the streets of republican Rome. With a prolonged breath of satisfaction I said to myself: 'Oh, here is life!' My vigor was redoubled in a few days. A lively desire for motion, a thing not habitual, took possession of me against my will. Without explaining it to myself, I went here and there, up and down, in order to observe, to learn, to inform myself and at night, returning to my room, I could have gone out again to walk still more. From this I understood why the Americans are so hard-working and untiring.*[8]

Thus, amid the unceasing publicity and social obligations, Salvini found time to see and begin to enjoy this new country he was to grow to love during his five American tours.

While in New York most of Salvini's time was taken up with rehearsals and performance oriented matters. As a result, little was written about his personal life in the American press. This lack of publicity was due no doubt to his inability to speak English, which became a barrier to Salvini's acceptance in the United States. Since Salvini could not speak English and was concerned about what was said of him in the American press, no personal interviews were published by the press after he began his performances. Therefore, Salvini, the man, was an "unknown" to his American admirers and little outside his biography as printed and published by Grau, his manager, was available to the American public during his tour.

The problem of language frequently surfaced in Salvini's reviews. After his final performance of *Othello*, the *New York Times* (23 October 1873, p. 5, col. 1) ran a second review of this production:

> *Critics handle the performances of American actors with very little regard to their reputations; but when a foreign artist appears, speaking or singing in a language they do not understand, and preceded by a reputation about which the critics know as little as they do of his native tongue, they endorse his reputation without looking in the face of it, and spin out articles of length and strength proportionate to a merit they take on trust. Come let us be honest! How many of those who witnessed the performance of M. Salvini knew what he was talking about!*

This was but the first of many similar comments made concerning Salvini's inability to speak English.

Because Salvini performed in Italian, a libretto was a necessity for his American audiences, especially for the unfamiliar foreign plays in his repertoire. In its assessment of Salvini's stay in Chicago, the *Chicago Tribune* (11 January 1874, p. 7, col. 2) clearly stated the problems American audiences faced in using these texts:

> *The libretto is a volume whose value cannot be duly estimated except at a Salvini performance. . . . For a greenback they [the audience] can purchase the privilege of describing what they have not seen nor even desired to see and can retail to their simpering lady friends the marvels of Salvini. . . . In addition to the text, it contains some wonderful stage directions which are calculated to mislead. The libretto says, "Conrad folds his arms and gazes on the floor," and the audience awaits in an agony of suspense to observe this marvel. Conrad, however, carefully abstains from doing anything of the kind, and, by the time the audience has realized his perfidious neglect of so essential an attitude, the play has moved along sometimes two pages.*

American audiences bought and used librettos even for the Shakespearean plays in his repertoire. These language centered problems were never overcome completely and haunted Salvini throughout his American tours.

Following a six week engagement in New York City, Salvini and his company went to Philadelphia where they played for two weeks. While there, Salvini saw E. L. Davenport play Hamlet. The *Chicago Daily Tribune* (7 December 1873, p. 6, col. 7) recorded their first meeting and also an incident with a Philadelphia photographer.

> *[I]t is reported that, as the curtain fell, he [Salvini] rushed behind the scenes, and, taking his brother artist in his arms, kissed him on both cheeks, exclaiming, 'Soul! Soul! Soul!' It is related, too, that, having had his photograph taken by Gutekunst, he was so pleased with the proof that he embraced the photographer warm-*

ly, to the no small alarm, however, of that gentleman, who had seen him in Othello, and remembered with a shudder his manner of dealing with Iago. Not understanding Italian, he thought with horror of his fate should the proof be unsatisfactory.

Since many of the press could not personally interview Salvini because of the language problem, many similar stories were printed in which the strength and emotionalism he exhibited in his acting were adapted to the known events of his personal life. These stories soon created Salvini's popular American image as an actor of physical strength and emotionality. It was not until his second American tour that Salvini, the man offstage, began to emerge.

Salvini's return to Philadelphia later in his tour brought to the fore the comparison of Forrest and Salvini as Othello. In an article entitled "Salvini's Rank As An Artist," the *Philadelphia Evening Bulletin* (21 November 1873, p. 4, col. 1-2) took its stand with Salvini:

Salvini never forgets the character he is playing. That is first and above all. Mr. Forrest remembered many times during a personation that he was Edwin Forrest and he forced his audiences to remember also. . . . The gift of genius was conferred upon both men, and each shaped a theory for himself. Whatever the respective value of the two theories, there is hardly room to doubt that Salvini's method of presenting his conception is that which commends itself more strongly to the majority of cultivated people.

In comparisons to other actors, both living and dead, Salvini was often considered the superior talent and his critical esteem, coupled with his growing popular image, quickly helped him win the support of the American public.

During this tour, Salvini made the acquaintance of many notable Americans who recorded their various impressions of the Italian actor. Henry Austin Clapp, the drama critic, saw Salvini perform in Boston and found his acting less intellectual than Edwin Booth's, "but in its mastery, . . . of the symbols of histrionic expression, it ranked, I think, above that of every other player whom the stage of America has known within the past fifty years."[9] Julia Ward Howe was impressed by Salvini, both as an actor and as a man. She gave a dinner-party for him and he became "a valued friend, always greeted with delight."[10] Henry Wadsworth Longfellow and Salvini developed a unique friendship. Longfellow could speak Italian and "took delight in speaking to [Salvini] with pure Tuscan."[11] William Dean Howells missed meeting Salvini at a dinner given by Longfellow and later wrote, "I still feel that I missed the best time of my life, and that I ought to be rewarded for my sacrifice."[12] Howells translated Ippolito d'Aste's *Samson* into an English version that Salvini used during his 1889 tour when he played with English speaking actors.

Among the stage personalities Salvini encountered during this tour was Clara Louise Kellogg, an operatic *prima donna*, who recorded her impressions of him in her *Memoirs*. Miss Kellogg and Salvini met frequently during

Salvini's American tours and these two artists developed a sincere admiration for one another.

> *It was my good fortune to know the elder Salvini in America. . . . He looked like a successful farmer; a very plain man, — very. He told me, among other interesting things, that no matter how small his part happened to be, he always played each succeeding act in a stronger colour, maintaining a steady* crescendo *so that the last impression of all was the climax.*[13]

The American actor Salvini most wanted to see perform was Edwin Booth. Booth was also on tour during the 1873-74 season and had written to Maurice Grau that he hoped to act *Hamlet* before Salvini "that I may in some slight degree manifest my respect for Signor Salvini, whom, unfortunately, I have been prevented from seeing. I trust that pleasure is yet in store for me. . . ."[14] In May, 1874, when Salvini played in Washington, D.C., he became aware that Booth was playing in Baltimore. With Grau's help, on 20 May, one of Salvini's days off, he went to see Booth play *Hamlet*. Salvini wrote in his autobiography that Booth "impersonated *Hamlet*, and *Hamlet* was Booth. . . . His long and wavy hair, large and expressive eyes, the movements of his young and supple body, accorded so well with the idea which by now all had made of the young prince of Denmark. The splendid diction and the penetrating philosophy which the phrases reveal, are in him the most notable quality."[15] In its review of Booth's performance, the *Baltimore Sun* (21 May 1874, p. 1, col. 7) noted that among "the spectators was Salvini, the Italian tragedian, who occupied a private box decorated for the occasion with the colors of his country." Salvini later saw Booth as Richelieu, Macbeth, and as Iago in *Othello*. He found Booth superb in the first two roles, but felt that Macbeth "did not suit his natures."[16] It was not until Salvini's fourth tour of America in 1886 that the famous joint appearances of Booth and Salvini in *Othello* and *Hamlet* occurred.

Salvini's response to Mardi Gras may not have helped his image of America nor assisted his publicity campaign. Pride in Italy and devotion to the Catholic church were made evident when he played in New Orleans during the Mardi Gras celebrations in 1874. His reactions to the city are probably his harshest toward any American metropolis: "The population of this city is divided between Catholics and Protestants, and, in my opinion, New Orleans is as they say: the spleen and the liver of the United States."[17] This reaction was caused, no doubt, by the impersonation of Pope Pius IX in the Mardi Gras parade. According to Salvini's description, the float representing Italy portrayed the Pope as giving his blessing to a band of brigands with knives in their mouths. That is not how the *New Orleans Daily Picayune* (18 February 1874, p. 2, col. 6) described the float: "The Pope sits enthroned with the keys of St. Peter in his grasp. On the right stands a bishop — on the left a Monk. In front, with bowed head and trustful glance, a gaily dressed Contadina, beside whom leans a swarthy dark-browed brigand. The front of the tableau was occupied with baptismal fonts and candelabras, emblems and suggestions of the Church's power and magnificence." Salvini took strong offense to this caricature and wrote the following letter to the carnival commission:

> *In the carnival procession, which took place Tuesday, February 17, representing the nations of two hemispheres, the masked figure of the Pope and the brigands should be understood to make a dispicable allusion to Italy. Every citizen has the obligation and right to rebel against a disgrace made to his country. The Italian residents in this city are offended and object to test the esteem, the sympathy and consideration of the generous citizens of New Orleans, for supposing that from these [feelings] can come the ill deserved insult; and [ask] if it [the city] can censure the inadvertence on the part of the secret society of the carnival, which is not free from blame and from contempt as they conceived the idea and carried it out. The Italy personified by the Pope and by the brigands is the Italy of the Jesuits, and of the renegades, the pests of human society. Italy, for the true Italian, ought to be represented by V. Emanuele, Gioberti, Cavour and Garibaldi. Every good Italian repels, protests, and scorns the offense made to a nation which, for ancient traditions and recent deeds, merits the respect and admiration of the civilized world; we are well convinced of finding an echo of support in this populace accustomed to render homage and justice to all who are noble and generous.*[18]

Thereafter, Salvini always resented this American city and played there only twice during his entire five tours.

A major barrier to Salvini's popular acceptance in America was his repertoire of little known Italian and French plays. Scripts for the first tour included Shakespeare's *Othello* and *Hamlet*, Giacometti's *Ingomar, La Morte Civile*, and *Elizabeth, the Queen*, Pellico's *Francisca Da Rimini*, Saumet's *The Gladiator*, Melesville's *Sullivan*, Alfieri's *Saul*, d'Aste's *Samson*, Voltaire's *Zaire* and Feuillet's *Romance of a Poor Young Man*. Almost all of Salvini's publicity centered on his performance as Othello and the American public wanted to see him perform this role rather than speaking Italian in plays most of them had neither heard of nor wanted to see. Because of the great emotional and physical demands of this role, Salvini refused to play Othello more than once a week and stipulated this in his contracts with Grau. The *Chicago Tribune* (8 February 1874, p. 7, col. 1) commented on Salvini's repertoire:

> *His European contracts, . . . always except the performance of* Othello, *which he deals out very sparingly. He only plays it on an average of eight times a year; and has broken through this rule in the United States only because of the comparative failure of his other pieces.*

Since Shakespeare was not very popular in Italy, Salvini's few performances of *Othello* in his homeland were to be expected. For the United States, however, where almost all of his advance publicity centered on this play, the demand to see him in this role should have been anticipated by both Grau and Salvini. The problem of the number of weekly performances of *Othello* haunted Salvini and every American manager he worked with during his five American tours.

Salvini had his greatest success with many famous figures in American theatrical and literary life and either became their friend or at least gained their praise. Joseph Jefferson III is quoted as saying that he thought "Salvini the greatest tragic actor he had ever seen," although he did not like the death-scene in *Othello* "where Salvini curls up like a beast."[19] E. L. Davenport granted that, in the context of Salvini's interpretation of Othello, the instances of poor taste seemed "all right and to the purpose."[20] Clara Morris, who worked with Salvini during a later tour, found his Othello too animalistic and "revolting, and with a shiver I exclaimed aloud, 'Ugh, you splendid brute!' "[21] Edward Robins admired Salvini's Othello because he felt it took "a man with a physique of a Salvini to give us the ideal Othello. Edwin Booth acted the part, but never looked it. Edwin Forrest looked the part, but, said his enemies, never acted it. Salvini acted and looked Othello."[22] Lester Wallack, when discussing actors' voices, decided "Brooke had the most powerful lungs, except Salvini's, that were ever given to an actor."[23] With leading American figures supporting Salvini, the public flocked to see him, especially when he played Othello, even though they could not understand him and were forced to follow the play in a libretto.

Salvini had established his reputation in Italy, Paris, Spain, Portugal and South America before he came to the United States in 1873. His first American tour was of paramount importance since a failure in North America could have prevented him from establishing a broad international reputation. He was the second Italian actor to attempt a tour of the United States, having been preceded by Ristori, and was the first actor from Italy to tour extensively the eastern half of America. Salvini was risking his career since both he and his company were relatively unknown in America and spoke a foreign language.

Salvini's visual style of acting, using many gestures and facial expressions, coupled with the emotional interpretation of his roles, made his acting in a foreign language generally acceptable to his American audiences, who responded to his actions more than to his incomprehensible language. Salvini's melodic voice with its magnificent projection, timbre and tone was a great asset to him when performing before American audiences that in part judged an actor upon his vocal abilities. The fact that he appeared during this first tour with strong Italian support helped to limit the criticisms of unknown scripts. It was only with the Shakespearean plays of his repertoire that any severe criticism appeared regarding his use of the Italian language. Nevertheless, with the support of leading American figures, his acting style and novel interpretations of Shakespeare's characters, Salvini overcame negative reaction and left the United States a popular and critical success.

Most importantly for Salvini, his American success led to an offer by Mapleson to appear in London and to tour England. His warm reception by the London critics further established his reputation in the English-speaking theatre. With his acceptance in England, France and the United States, Salvini joined the ranks of actors with international reputations.

Although his five tours (1873-74; 1880-81; 1882-83; 1885-86; 1889-90) were complicated by problems with managers, support, role interpretations and language, Salvini was one of the most successful foreign actors to play in America during the period of 1873-1890. In addition he played longer on the American stage than any other foreign language speaking actor. Artistically, Salvini's acting of *Othello, The Gladiator*, and *Samson* were considered by many North American critics as the best ever seen on the stage. Although American critics often quarrelled over Salvini's interpretations of his roles (especially those of Shakespeare), they praised his acting abilities almost to a man. Salvini's acting received acclaim from Towse of the *New York Evening Post*, Dithmar of the *New York Times*, Clapp of the *Boston Advertiser*, Fuller and Copeland of the *Boston Post*, Apthorp of the *Boston Transcript*, William T. M. Ball of the *Boston Daily Evening Traveller* and even from Edwin Forrest's staunch supporter, James Rees (better known under the pseudonym of "Colley Cibber") and Edwin Booth's admirer and friend, William Winter of the *New York Tribune*. His series of joint appearances with Clara Morris (1883) and Edwin Booth (1886) were artistic and historic high points of his tours. The Booth-Salvini engagement was considered one of the greatest artistic events of the late nineteenth century American theatre by many American critics including William Winter, Henry Austin Clapp and John Ranken Towse. Yet, even with this critical support, the name of Salvini has almost been lost in accounts of American theatre history.

During the 1880's, the United States, just over one hundred years old, was developing a stronger sense of its identity as a leading nation of the world and this realization was expressed in all aspects of American life. Congress passed legislation which curtailed foreign immigration as the American people began to emphasize their national heritage. This same spirit of national pride was increasingly evident in the American theatre. Before and during Salvini's fifth tour, a small group of actors demanded that only American actors perform on American stages. This group was vocal, received newspaper publicity across the United States and likely had some influence on how the American critics perceived foreign stars. Salvini's critics increasingly found him "Italianate" and "Southern," thereby segregating him from the stage traditions of the English-speaking theatre in the United States.

The memory of Salvini as an international starring actor has also been dimmed by other factors. Because of the poor artistic and financial state of the Italian theatre during the last half of the nineteenth century, Salvini was forced to make his name as a foreign star in countries with a strong and active theatre — England, France and the United States. Because he was Italian, however, he was never considered an integral part of the theatre of these countries and, therefore, had no strong national support. Also, with the emergence of realism during the last decade of the nineteenth century, Salvini's Shakespearean and basically tragic repertoire quickly placed him among the actors of the classical rather than the realistic school of acting and drama. As a result, he quickly lost his place in the mainstream of the theatrical world. Another factor to be considered was the conservative lifestyle led by Salvini. He was an emotional Italian actor on stage, but, outside the theatre, he was a humble father and husband who led a rather simple life centered on his family. Salvini's personal life was in few ways as flamboyant as the drinking of Edwin Booth, the menagerie and art collection of Sara Bernhardt or the affairs of Lillie Langtry. Thus, Salvini, who lacked strong national support, made his name famous with a classical repertoire and lived a simple life, has received less recognition in theatre history than his English, French and American contemporaries.

NOTES

[1]*Dearest Isa: Robert Browning's Letters to Isabella Blagden* (Austin, 1951), p. 25.

[2]*The Letters of Elizabeth Barrett Browning*, ed. Frederic G. Kenyon, vol. II (London, 1898), p. 319. These letters refer to the time when Salvini and Clementaina Cazzola left the Dondini Company; it also was the time Garibaldi was fighting to free Italy from the Bourbons.

[3]William W. Story, *Roba Di Roma*, vol. I (London, 1963), p. 206-208.

[4]Van Wyck Brooks, *The Dream of Arcadia: American Writers and Artists in Italy 1760-1915* (New York), 1958, p. 101.

[5]Tommaso Salvini, *Ricordi, Aneddoti Ed Impressioni Dell'Artista Tommaso Salvini* (Milano, 1895), p. 280.

[6]*Ibid.*, p. 280-281.

[7]*Celso Salvini, Tommaso Salvini Nella Storia Del Teatro E Nella Vita Del Suo Tempo* (Bologna, 1955), p. 274.

[8]Tommaso Salvini, *Ricordi*, p. 281-282.

[9]Henry Austin Clapp, *Reminiscences of a Dramatic Critic* (Boston, 1902), p. 143-145.

[10]Laura E. Richards and Maude Howe Elliott, *Julia Ward Howe (1819-1910)* (Boston, 1916), p. 351.

[11]Tommaso Salvini, *Ricordi*, p. 283.

[12]William D. Howells, *Literary Friends and Acquaintances*, vol. 32 (Bloomington, 1968), p. 173.

[13]Clara Louise Kellogg, *Memoirs of an American Prima Donna* (New York, 1913), p. 283.

[14]Edwina Booth Grossman, *Edwin Booth: Recollections by His Daughter* (London, 1894), p. 182.

[15]Tommaso Salvini, *Ricordi*, p. 352.

[16]*Ibid.*

[17]*Ibid.*, p. 284.

[18]*Ibid.*, p. 284-285.

[19]*Letters of Richard Watson Gilder*, ed. by Rosamond Gilder (Boston, 1916), p. 68.

[20]Carol Jones Carlisle, *Shakespeare From the Greenroom: Actors' Criticisms of Four Major Tragedies* (Chapel Hill, 1969), p. 203.

[21]*Ibid.*

[22]Edward Robins, *Twelve Great Actors* (New York, 1900), p. 16-17.

[23]Lester Wallack, *Memories of Fifty Years* (New York, 1889), p. 45.

Sándor Hevesi in 1906.

Sándor Hevesi and the Thália Society in Hungary

PÉTER SZAFKÓ

Sándor Hevesi (1873-1939) was the first outstanding representative of the modern Hungarian theatre. Not merely a stage director, he was the first Hungarian to perfect a high-quality repertory system and to insist on the unity of all aspects of theatrical activity in the production of plays. Hevesi opened a new phase in the history of the National Theatre and the Opera House, laid down the theoretical bases of modern acting in Hungary, introduced the works of such prominent playwrights as Ibsen and Shaw, worked out a new style for the productions of Shakespeare's plays, translated dozens of English, German and French dramas, and it was Hevesi who made the Hungarian theatre known in the Western world. The first important phase of his career was his directorship of the Thália Society. Since his work with the Thália deeply influenced all his future activities, it is necessary to examine the role the Thália Society played in Hevesi's theatrical career.

Sándor Hevesi was only seventeen when he began his career as a theatre critic, and from the beginning his main concern was the artistic quality of the National Theatre of Budapest. This was quite natural since the National Theatre has always been one of the most significant means of expressing national consciousness and Hungarian culture. Since its establishment in 1837, the National Theatre has been operated on a repertory basis and has, consequently, been a good indicator of both official and public taste.

When Hevesi began to write theatrical criticism in the 1890s, the National Theatre was in a decline, and the young critic courageously attacked the commercialism penetrating the theatre's activity. Hevesi had his own idea of what a theatre should be, and in his reviews he not only evaluated the performances but also gave expression to his ideals. He was young and relatively inexperienced in theatrical matters, yet his criticism proved that he was a good theoretician, as evidenced by the publication of his first book, *Drama and the Stage*. The book is one of the first theoretical studies of its kind in Hungary, and only the beginning of a long series of studies in acting and directing focusing on the relationship between the written play and its actual performance, and many other crucial topics previously neglected by Hungarian scholars.[1]

As a result of Hevesi's critical and theoretical activities, László Beöthy, the manager of the National Theatre in 1901, suggested that the young critic

Péter Szafkó is Assistant Professor at the Lajos Kossuth University in Debrecen, Hungary. He is presently a visiting professor in the Department of Uralic and Altaic Studies at Indiana University.

A scene from a 1908 production of Irma Madách's *The Tragedy of Man* directed by Hevesi.

join the theatre as a director. Hevesi eagerly accepted this opportunity to become involved in the practical aspects of acting and directing. His dedication to serious production work at this time provided him with the artistic principles upon which he based his later theories.

Little is known concerning the details of Hevesi's early directing ventures. We do know, however, that before the staging of a play in a foreign translation, Hevesi would correct mistakes in earlier translations, sometimes resulting in his own translation of the play. In 1903 he directed his first Shakespearean comedy, *Much Ado About Nothing* (15 April 1903, National Theatre). Since the National Theatre had produced the play in such a way that it seemed long and confusing, Hevesi decreased the number of the scenes and made several alterations to make the script more appropriate for a Hungarian audience.

In 1904 three university students — Marcell Benedek, Gyorgy Lukács, and László Bánóczi — asked Hevesi to be the leading director of a new theatrical enterprise, the Thália Society. Although he remained at the National Theatre, he devoted his time to this completely new and exciting work. It would provide him the possibility to carry out his own theatrical plans.

The Thália Society was the first Hungarian independent theatre founded on the examples of Antoine's Théatre Libre, Otto Brahm's Freie Bühne, and Stanislavsky's Moscow Art Theatre. "This society, which was not commercial in its aims, numbered among its members many ambitious and talented young actors, writers and painters, and the plays produced, unhampered by tradition, were works of a higher order."[2] The main objective of the Thália was "to give adequate expression to the dramas of Ibsen, Strindberg, Gorky, and others."[3] The Society's slogan was "Truth in playwriting — truth in acting," by which Hevesi and the others meant that they would produce only plays which represented "real life" with realistic characters involved in actual social problems. Gyorgy Székely in his paper, "The 'Thalia Society', 1904-08; The Summing-Up of Contemporary Trends in the Hungarian Theatre," delivered at the Fifth International Congress on Theatre Research in Budapest in 1967, pointed out six main principles which served as "leit-motifs" in the nearly five-year activity of the Thália Society: "First: to build up a repertory of a very high literary and artistic level; second: to reject all pathetism, all conventional routine work in acting; third: to be liberal in style but always taking care of reality, of psychological genuineness; fourth: to train a new, intelligent generation of actors and producers; fifth: to create a new audience; and last but not least: to be true to the highest ideals in the world of theatre arts."[4]

Of the thirty-five plays produced by the Thália, twenty-five were directed by Hevesi. They included such important plays of the modern theatre as Ibsen's *The Master Builder, A Doll's House*, and *Wild Duck*, Hauptmann's *Elga*, Gorky's *Lower Depths*, and others, several of which were first performed in Hungary.[5] The social reformers in Hungary recognized the significance of the Thália Society and it received the intellectual support of such prominent figures as Zoltán Kodály, the world-famous composer, and Béla Balázs, Hungary's best-known film critic and theoretician. At the same

Hevesi's library.

time, however, the Thália was also a theatre for the people, frequently performing plays in the union halls of workers. Although authorities claimed these various facilities in which they performed would create a fire hazard and banned further performances in 1908, the activity of the first modern Hungarian theatre, the Thália Society, having produced a number of eminent actors, actresses, and directors, who later worked in the leading theatre of Budapest, had become "the cradle of the whole Hungarian theatrical art of the 20th Century."[6]

The Thália Society served Hevesi as an experimental workshop as well as a school. In his first book, *Drama and the Stage*, he laid down his basic ideas of dramatic and theatrical art but to turn these theories, however practically oriented they were, into practice required much effort. Since the Thália Society lacked a permanent stage, Hevesi always had to consider the changing physical arrangements of each new building. In 1908, when the Society was forced to discontinue its unparalleled activity, Hevesi published two books: *The Art of Acting*[7] and *The Art of Performing*[8] in which he summed up the theoretical results of his practical achievements and experiments. While working with the Thália, Hevesi also initiated a school for young actors which proved instrumental in the training of a new generation of performers. A considerable number of the leading actors, actresses, and directors coming into the forefront in the twenties and thirties were former students of Hevesi's.

As a regisseur, Hevesi opposed the singular domination of the stage director as, for example, Reinhardt insisted, and instead claimed that a performance should be the unity of the script, the acting, and the atmosphere required. He was the first Hungarian director to emphasize that a good production could be the result of long, collective work. At a time when the usual number of rehearsals at other theatres totaled from five to ten, the premiere of Ibsen's *Wild Duck* (25 December 1906) by the Thália Society was the culmination of forty-seven rehearsals.

Hevesi cannot be classified on the basis of one artistic trend or experimentation with various production techniques since he combined characteristics from many artists including Craig, Stanislavsky, etc. Most significant for Hevesi was the creation of a perfect stage illusion, a proper atmosphere for the play, psychological realism, and a unified performance. Though realism remained his ultimate artistic goal, it was more important for him to be faithful to the essence of the drama. Thus, in Lawrence Alma Tadema's *The Invisible Helmsman* (17 December 1905, Thália) he used a mystical and lyrical setting to reflect the gloomy atmosphere of the play, and symbolic elements pervaded the production's of *The Wild Duck* and D'Annunzio's *Dead City* (24 March 1907, Thália). Before he produced Gorky's *Lower Depths* (27 January 1907, Thália), he obtained Stanislavsky's original stage production book which he believed greatly aided him. The Thália performance, however, was not an imitation of the Russian director's concept. Hevesi combined his own idea of Gorky's drama with ideas from Stanislavsky.

As a result of his attempts to create a perfect unity on the stage, Hevesi realized the importance of ensemble acting. He emphasized perfect timing of movement for all actors in a group scene to achieve the illusion of reality.

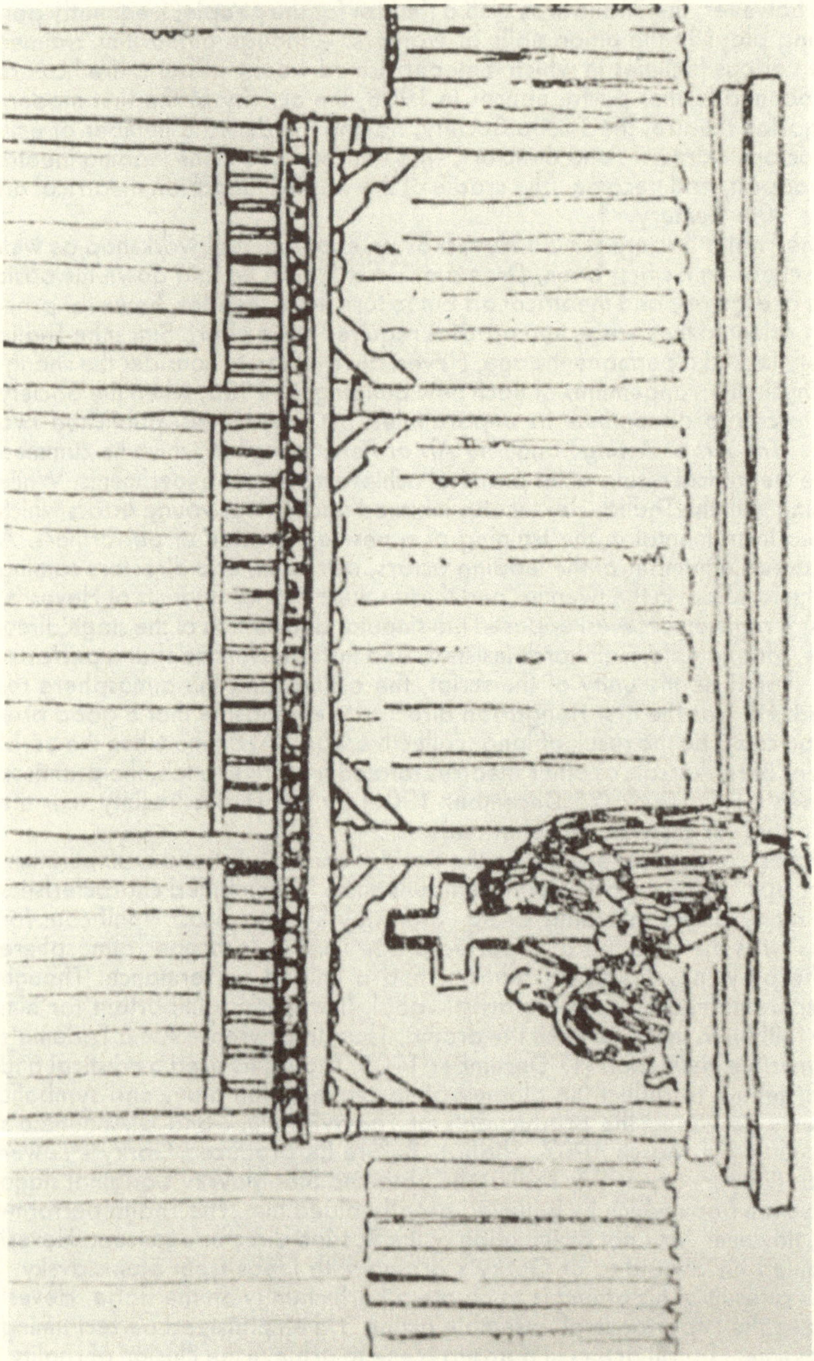

Stage design for *Hamlet* on a recreated Elizabethan stage directed by Hevesi at the National Theatre in 1911.

He gained a reputation as a "master" of group scenes, an unusual compliment for that period. During his directorship of the Thália Society, Hevesi made friends with Eward Gordon Craig, who considered him one of the outstanding and promising regisseurs of Europe. To show his respect for Hevesi, Craig asked him to write an introduction for his new book, *On The Art of the Theatre*.[9]

Hevesi was as much a theoretician and a literary scholar as a stage director, and he always maintained more than one field of interest. While working with the Thália, he also directed nine plays at the National Theatre and eleven productions at the Népszíház-Vígopera (People's Theatre — Musical Theatre). His production choices in this period demonstrated a broad range of styles. In addition to the already mentioned contemporary plays, his repertoire included Bizet's *Carmen*, three comedies by Moliere, and two operettas. In 1908 he first directed *The Tragedy of Man* by Imre Madách, a classical Hungarian drama which was a constant artistic challenge to his regisseurial skills after he had become director of the National Theatre in 1922.[10]

Apart from directing a great number of plays at various theatres, Hevesi wrote numerous essays on different topics, ranging from Hungarian literature to the dramatic art of Shakespeare to book reviews.[11] He was the first Hungarian theatrical figure to become a contributor to the international journal, *The Mask*, edited by Edward Gordon Craig. This publication served as an important forum where the prominent European directors of the time expressed their opinions on various questions concerning theatrical productions and theories. In *The Mask* Hevesi published an article on "Shakespeare as Scenographer" in which he raised the question: "Is not a return to the Shakespearian stage a rather hopeless task if one considers the majority of the spectators?"[12] Shakespeare was one of his favorite classic playwrights, and he maintained that the British poet's plays should be produced in a proper way to meet the demands of the contemporary audience. He published his first article on Shakespeare in 1900 and after that he wrote essays on the connection between his plays and the stage, on his influence in the development of acting, on the reception of his plays in Hungary, as well as numerous essays on his individual dramas. In 1919 he published *The Real Shakespeare and Other Questions*, a summary of all his previous studies on Shakespeare.[13]

Although Hevesi and the leaders of the Thália Society planned to produce Shakespeare's plays, the early banning of the theatre thwarted it. Thus, not until 1911 could Hevesi first apply a so-called "re-created" Elizabethean stage for his *Hamlet* production (5 May 1911, National Theatre). He experimented with the concept throughout his career and it obtained considerable critical success. He considered Shakespeare so important in a theatre repertory that, after having been appointed director of the National Theatre, he at once produced three cycles of his plays in June, October, and November-December, 1923, including *Twelfth Night, Hamlet, A Midsummernight's Dream, King Lear, Richard III, Macbeth, Julius Caesar, Henry IV, Much Ado About Nothing* (on a re-created stage), *The Merchant of Venice, Romeo and Juliet*, and *The Tempest*. J. T. Grein, the well-known

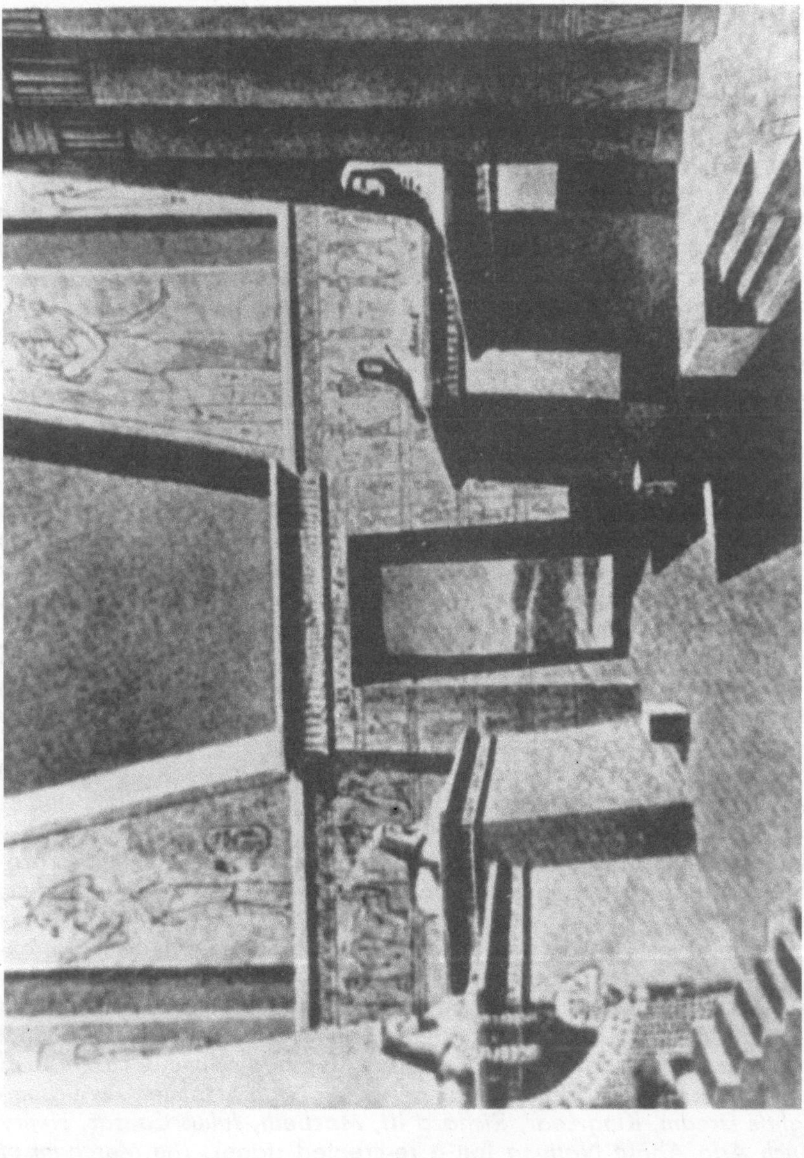

Stage design for Verdi's *Aida* directed by Hevesi at the Opera House in 1913.

English theatre director visited Hungary in 1924, and, after returning to England, wrote a series of articles on the Hungarian stage for the *Illustrated London News* and stated that Hevesi's productions were even more Shakespearean than those performed in the Old Vic of London. "If I were richly endowed with the world's goods, my first mission would be to transfer the Shakespeare Cycle from the National Theatre of Budapest to London, lock, stock, and barrel. — To what heights could we not fly, had we but one Hevesi in London!"[14]

Whatever Hevesi learned from his experiences and, experiments for the Thália, he applied later in his career. Between 1912 and 1914 Hevesi was the main director of the Royal Opera House of Budapest, and these two years proved to be one of the most flourishing periods of the theatre. Not only was Hevesi the first to direct Verdi's *Aida,* completely sung in Hungarian (13 November 1913, Opera House), but he also built a repertory of high artistic quality. At the same time, however, Hevesi realized that it was very important to gain a larger audience for opera productions and therefore included several light operas in his repertoire. As a result the Opera House became more popular than ever before. This was undoubtedly a consequence of the policy of the Thália Society, the first Hungarian theatre to produce plays regularly for a working class audience. Furthermore, even when directing operas, Hevesi attempted and, in most cases, succeeded in creating a unified atmosphere of the dramatic and musical elements as well as the acting and singing.

After two-year's work at the Opera, Hevesi believed he had acquired enough experience in directing operas and decided to return to the National Theatre. During 1915-1922 he produced thirty-one plays, wrote two dramas, four comedies and an operetta libretto (with Zsolt Harsányi), and authored more than twenty articles on dramatic and theatrical theories and practice, including his famous study on *The Real Shakespeare and Other Questions*. In addition he published several articles in German and French periodicals. He translated a number of foreign plays and adapted a number of famous Hungarian novels for the stage, became the only rightful Hungarian translator of G. B. Shaw, who admired the activity of this Hungarian man of the theatre.

All in all, by 1922 Hevesi had become the leading personality of the Hungarian Theatre. With his reputation as theorist, essayist, director, translator, and playwright well established, it was quite natural that he was appointed director of the National Theatre, the most prestigious theatre in the country.

As a director, his most important achievement was the establishment of a repertory policy of high standards which has been a characteristic feature of the National Theatre during its flourishing periods. Not surprisingly, the National Theatre reached its peak under Sándor Hevesi's directorship as a result of his systematic production of classical and contemporary foreign and Hungarian plays. He established the so-called "cycles" of dramas by such playwrights as Shakespeare, Moliere, and of a special Hungarian dramatic genre, the *népszínmű* (folk-play). In 1924 Hevesi opened the

Chamber Theatre of the National Theatre, where such plays as Pirandello's *The Pleasure of Honesty* (Hungarian premiere; 11 November 1924). Shaw's *You Never Can Tell*(19 December 1925), Ibsen's *John Gabriel Borkman* (7 April 1928), and Chekhov's *The Sea Gull* (22 January 1930), etc. were produced. The whole concept of the Chamber Theatre, and especially its repertory, was very similar to the Thália Society.

In 1927 Hevesi began his teaching career at the Actors' Academy where his lectures on stage direction and acting may be considered to be the continuance of his work during the Thália period.

By 1932, however, the financial situation of the National Theatre had become critical and those critics who had been against his basically non-commercial and artistically high quality repertory policy felt it was time to replace him. Hevesi left the theatre in October 1932 to join the Magyar Theatre where he worked until he died in 1939.

Although Hevesi was internationally known in his own time, and "played the same part in the development of the Budapest theatre as Antoine did earlier in Paris, Brahm in Berlin, Grein in London, and Stanislavsky in Moscow," later histories of the world theatre rarely mention him.[15] John Kardoss, the Hungarian theatre historian, may have been right when he said that "owing to the isolation of the Hungarian language, the truly great ones (i.e. Hungarian theatrical persons) have never had a chance to win the admiration of civilized mankind like some of their more fortunate French, Italian, English, American or German colleagues had."[16] Sándor Hevesi can well be ranked as the greatest Hungarian director of this century.

NOTES

[1]Sándor Hevesi, *Dráma és színpad* (Budapest: Singer és Wolfer, 1896).

[2]P. "Budapest," *The Mask*, 1, No. 3-4 (May-June 1908), 87.

[3]Bela Kiralyfalvi, *The Aesthetics of Gyorgy Lukacs* (Princeton: Princeton University Press, 1975), p.5.

[4]György Székely, "The 'Thalia Society', 1904-08; The Summing-Up of Contemporary Trends in the Hungarian Theatre," *Theatre Research — Recherches Théâtrales*, 10, No. 2 (1969), 113.

[5]Most of the data used in the article are taken from Anna László, *Hevesi Sándor* (Budapest: Gondolat, 1973).

[6]Geza Hegedűs and Judit Kónya, *A magyar dráma útja* [The Development of the Hungarian Drama] (Budapest: Gondolat, 1964), p. 143. My translation.

[7]Sándor Hevesi, *A Színjátszás művész* (Budapest: Stampfel, 1908).

[8]Sándor Hevesi, *Az előadás művézete* (Budapest: Stampfel, 1908).

[9]Edward Gordon Craig, *On the Art of the Theatre* (London, 1912), pp. xiii-xiv.

[10]First production: 16 June 1908; second: 22 January 1923; third: 30 October 1926; fourth: 1 September 1929; all in the National Theatre.

[11]For a complete bibliography of his works and plays directed, see László, pp. 343-422.

[12]Alexander [Sándor] Hevesi, "Shakespeare as Scenographer," *The Mask*, 2, No. 1-3 (July 1909), 6-8.

[13]Sándor Hevesi, *Az igazi Shakespeare és egyéb kérdések* (Budapest: Táltos, 1919).

[14]J. T. Grein, "The World of the Theatre," *London Illustrated News*, 29 November 1924, p. 1030.

[15]John Kardoss, *Hungarian Theatre to the Twentieth Century* (New York: Long Island University, 1967), p. 19.

[16]Ibid., p. 18.

Notes and Queries

Edwin Booth's Performances: New Documentation

DANIEL J. WATERMEIER

In the Harvard Theatre Collection are a set of hitherto unreported manuscripts catalogued as "M. Isabella Stone . . . *Commentaries on Edwin Booth*" (MS thr 219*68M-89). The Stone Commentaries actually consist of three separate documents:

1. *A Booth-Winter edition of* Othello *(1878) interleaved with over 200 pages of holograph notes on Booth's Iago.*
2. *A Booth-Winter edition of* Hamlet *(5th edition, 1881) interleaved with over 200 pages of holograph notes on Booth's Hamlet.*
3. *A small handmade "book", about 4"x5½", constructed of folded and sewn sheets of paper, containing several pages of holograph notes on both Booth's Othello and King Lear.*

The Commentaries were donated to Harvard in 1968 by Leslie H. Levinson, a used-book dealer in Framingham, Massachusetts, who in turn had acquired them in a parcel of books and papers she bought from an antique dealer.[1]

Little is known about "M. Isabella Stone." She is undoubtedly one Mary Isabella Stone, born in Framingham on January 24, 1850, the daughter of Henry Orne Stone (1818-1909), a physician who practiced in Framingham from about 1850 until his death, and Mary Baldwin Lowe (1817-1891). Mary Isabella graduated from the State Normal School in Framingham (now Framingham State College) in July, 1870. She was appointed a "practice school teacher" at the Normal School in September 1870, but resigned at the end of the academic year. She never married. Levinson has some manuscript essays which indicate that among Stone's pastimes was hiking in the New Hampshire mountains. Apart from the Commentaries, however, none of her papers are related to the theatre. There is no other information about her life. She died on September 28, 1921. At the time of her death, her address was 999 Worcester Road, Framingham, apparently a home for the aged.[2]

The Stone Commentaries are significant documents, providing a wealth of fresh insights into Booth's performances in several major roles. Without reproducing the entire series of manuscripts, it is impossible to describe all of Stone's annotations, but perhaps a brief general description of their con-

Daniel J. Watermeier is Professor of Theatre at SUNY-Plattsburgh.

tents will serve to indicate their value to students of Booth, of the American theatre, or of Shakespearean stage history.[3]

Stone made her notes at various Booth performances in Boston in the early 1880's. She meticulously recorded the date of each performance. Her King Lear and Othello notes are dated respectively November 9 and November 12, 1883, the Globe Theatre. She indicates that she saw Booth's Iago on several occasions: on March 13 and March 27, 1880 and on December 10, 1881 at the Park Theatre, and then on February 20, 1884 at the Globe Theatre. She even distinguishes her comments on Booth's 1880-1881 Iago performances from her comments on his 1884 performance by marking the latter with a number or "dot" in blue pencil.

Stone records that she saw Booth as Hamlet a half-dozen times as follows: November 1, 1879 at the Grand Opera House in New York; March 13, 1880 and December 17 and 31, 1881 at the Park Theatre; and November 24, 1883 and February 23, 1884 at the Globe Theatre. Like so many other playgoers of the era, she was greatly impressed by Booth's Hamlet. She saw his Hamlet the first time, she writes, for "enchantment"; the second time for "impressions and recollections"; the third time for "criticism"; and finally the fourth time for "comparison." Although Stone seems unable to count, she explains that the "first time she saw Booth hardly counted for criticism" so her record actually begins from the second time she saw him.

The bulk of her Hamlet notes are drawn from her observations in 1880 and 1881, while her annotations of Booth's 1883 and 1884 performances aim at noting differences, changes, or refinements in the earlier performances. Stone distinguishes these latter entries by marking the 1883 notes with a green pencil and the 1884 notes with a red pencil.

Stone's Commentaries on Booth's Hamlet and Iago are essentially moment-by-moment, often line-by-line descriptions of Booth's vocal interpretations, movements, gestures, and facial expressions in these two celebrated roles. They include detailed descriptions of Booth's costumes, jewelry, personal properties, even makeup. Stone also often gives her highly personal reaction to the effect of Booth's acting at key moments in his performances. In fact, Stone's notes offer the only detailed feminine view of Booth's acting, a view undoubtedly shared by the many women, young and old, who flocked to Booth's performances throughout his career.[4]

Booth's Hamlet has, of course, been fully reconstructed by Charles H. Shattuck in his splendid *The Hamlet of Edwin Booth* (1969). Shattuck based his work on various documents, but in particular on the Charles W. Clarke manuscript, a very detailed scene-by-scene, line-by-line eyewitness account of Booth's 1870 Hamlet. Regrettably, the Stone Commentaries were acquired only after Shattuck had completed his work; otherwise, I am certain they would have been used to complement, corroborate, and supplement the Clarke Manuscript.[5]

The Stone and Clarke manuscripts are similar enough in form to beg some general comparison. Stone's Commentaries document Booth's Hamlet a decade later than the Clarke record, during the period immediately before and after his important tours of Great Britain and Germany in the early

1880's. Booth was older, middle-aged in fact, but probably at the very peak of his histrionic power and popularity.

Stone's account is not quite as full as Clarke's, nor is it as "systematic." For example, unlike Clarke, she does not methodically record vocal accents, pauses, or variations in pitch, rhythm, or colorations. Like Clarke, Stone aimed to describe as concretely as possible what she saw and heard, but her observations are more "impressionistic" and less "technical" than Clarke's. She writes that she wanted especially to capture Hamlet's "train of thought" (her expression), that complex web of feelings underpinning Booth's characterization. Clarke saw Booth's Hamlet eight times between January 18 and March 19, 1870. His record is a composite account of these performances. Stone documents Booth's performance in several different years, noting significant changes in business, costuming, and interpretation from year to year. As such, it is a "comparative" rather than a "composite" record.

Stone's Hamlet Commentary does not significantly alter the image of Booth's Hamlet reconstructed for us by Shattuck after Clarke. It does, however, deepen, enrich and fine tune the vision with additional descriptive details; and sometimes it does offer new, different, even rather surprising accounts of Booth's business, interpretation, and costuming in the role.

Stone, for example, records that Booth, who generally appeared *au naturel* as Hamlet, eschewing a wig even after he turned grey, wore for his 1883 performance in Boston "a long curly wig of auburn chestnut color" and "a faint mustache!" Much to Stone's disappointment, his interpretation and business also seemed "more youthful" in keeping with this new physical appearance.[6] Several other notes imply that Booth during this period, after over twenty-five years of playing Hamlet, was perhaps exploring a new direction for his most celebrated role.

Stone's notes on Booth's Iago are the most detailed extant eyewitness descriptions of his performances in this role. They substantially and significantly augment the record of "The Victorian theatre's finest interpretation of the Iago problem."[7] While Booth's Iago has been studied by contemporary scholars, it has not been reconstructed in the same detail as his Hamlet. But with the riches of the Stone Commentaries as the key document, such a detailed reconstruction would now be possible.[8]

Stone's "book" of notes on Booth's Othello and King Lear was probably her "workbook" in which she jotted her observations and ideas either during or immediately after a performance. She then undoubtedly intended to recopy these notes into the appropriate Booth-Winter editions at a later time, perhaps refining and reorganizing them in the process. But Stone either did not recopy these notes, or if she did, the manuscript has been lost.

Her Othello Commentaries contain vivid descriptions of Booth's costumes for Acts I, II, III, and IV and a moment-by-moment, often line-by-line record of Booth's voice, facial expressions, movements, business, and general interpretation for the last climactic act only. Once again, these notes significantly augment the data available from other primary sources, such as Booth's promptbooks.

Stone seems to have intended not to fully annotate Booth's King Lear performance, but rather, as she herself writes, to describe only the "special parts" which were the "most touching," "vivid," or "electrical." Thus, her King Lear commentaries contain only a few line-by-line descriptions of the Lear-Poor Tom scene (III, iv) and the "recognition scene," (IV, vii) but these few notes are very concrete and revealing.

The force of Booth's acting has long since passed from living memory, but now thanks to the zeal of Mary Isabella Stone some of its forgotten glories are restored.

NOTES

[1]Letter from Levinson, September 2, 1981.

[2]J. Gardner Bartlett, *Gregory Stone Genealogy: Ancestry and Descendents of Dean Gregory Stone of Cambridge, Mass., 1320-1917* (Boston, 1918), pp. 355-356.; Letter from Sarah A. Phillips, Special Collections Librarian and Archivist, Wittemore Library, Framingham State College, September 1, 1981. Letters to other descendents of the Henry Stone family revealed no further information.

[3]I am currently preparing a longer essay describing Stone's Commentaries in some detail. It will be released for publication later this year.

[4]Booth was always, even towards the end of his career, something of a "matinée idol". Preserved at The Players are dozens of notes to Booth from women admirers — offers of marriage and assignation, as well as simple and sincere appreciations of his artistry — that attest to his distaff popularity.

[5]I brought the Stone manuscripts to the attention of Professor Shattuck in the Spring of 1981.

[6]See Shattuck, pp. 306-307. Stone's notes in this matter are corroborated by a review in the Boston *Herald* of November 20, 1883 which also mentions the new "shadow of a mustache" and "locks of a light brown hue."

[7]Marvin Rosenburg in *The Masks of Othello* (1961), pp. 128-134. See also Arthur Colby Sprague's essay on Booth's Iago in *Shakespearian Players* and *Performances* (1953), pp. 121-135.

[8]Other important resources would include Booth's numerous notes on Iago which he contributed to Horace Howard Furness' Variorum *Othello* (1886), the extant Booth *Othello* promptbooks, and dozens of contemporary reviews and reminiscenses of his performances.

Feature Section: Theatre History Obscurities

Theatre History Obscurities will feature the visual reproduction of a wide variety of theatre related items from libraries, institutes, museums, and private collections that have not previously been published or are not readily available.

A 1848 caricature scene of an enthusiastic audience greeting the appearance of Jenny Lind in Hamburg. Photo reproduction courtesy a private collection.

A publicity flyer for Fritz Leiber's 1934-35 season. Leighton and Leffler booking agency. Photo reproduction courtesy a private collection.

A 1920's promotion flyer for Fritz Leiber in the role of Hamlet. Photo reproduction courtesy a private collection. (Note: The Fritz Leiber Collection is located at the University of Illinois.)

A fan honoring Rose McClendon in a Black Leadership series. The back of the fan has printed the name of a funeral home in Louisiana. Photo reproduction courtesy a private collection.

Close-up of insert on Black Leadership fan.

A "Theatrical" elevated tank design by Abram E. Neff submitted in the 1931 competition to develop aesthetic improvement in the character of elevated steel water tanks. Sponsored by the Chicago Bridge and Iron Works. Photo reproduction courtesy a private collection.

Scene from the souvenir program for the Klaw and Erlanger touring production of *Ben Hur*, circa 1900. Photo courtesy Harold J. Nichols.

Theatre History Crossword Puzzle

FELICIA HARDISON LONDRÉ

CLUES

ACROSS

1. Swedish time capsule
10. Last word in the title of Lillian Mortimer's best-known melodrama
11. The Japenese know how it's done.
12. Where Serafina keeps Rosario's ashes
14. Berlin literary journal that first described Romanticism, *Das Athena---*
15. Sheridan Whiteside learns what you can't take with you.
16. Spanish for dada
18. Where Wagner created a mystic chasm
22. Congreve used this word twice in one three-word play title.
24. *The --menides* by Aeschylus
25. First name of playwright jailed for her 1926 play with risqué title
26. Actress _____ Worth
28. Initials of man who runs Eugene O'Neill National Playwrights Conference
29. Jerome Savary's Grand _____ Circus
31. Style of Greek comedy
33. Primate in hirsute American play
34. Where this journal is published (Abbrev.)
35. Politicizer of opera
36. Director of Saxe-Meiningen troupe
40. Initials of *Ralph Roister Doister*'s author
41. *DuBarry --- a Lady*, but was Ethel Merman?
42. *-- the Hawk's Well*
44. "- ---- in shekels," says Neil Simon.
47. Daddy of Dada
48. *---- Royal* by Montherlant
50. Pseudonym of *Nicholas Nickleby* author
51. Theatre on the Boulevard of Crime

DOWN

1. A divine ending for a play
2. Designer of *Pie in the Sky* (1941)
3. The beginning of theatre
4. She had an on-again off-again relationship with Hanswurst.
5. *---- la Douce*
6. Initials of author of *Arnaldo da Brescia* (1843)
7. Play by David Storey
8. *--! Calcutta!*
9. Title role performed by Helene Weigel in 1949
13. Home of Trinity Square Repertory Company (Abbrev.)
15. Labiche's farcical straw hat
17. Character in *Prometheus Bound* who was tormented by a gadfly
19. How you pay for theatre tickets in Japan
20. Lope who invented the *paso*
21. Initials of American character actress who appeared in stage and film versions of *Summer and Smoke*
23. First three letters of a title of a play by Roger Vitrac (1928)
27. Endless play by Samuel Beckett
30. ---ra Behn
32. Initials of melodramatic American actor-manager
34. Massinger's way to pay old debts
37. Greek theatrical headdresses
38. Initials of Craig's collaborator on 1911 *Hamlet*
39. Italian funny business

Theatre History Crossword Puzzle

by Felicia Hardison Londré

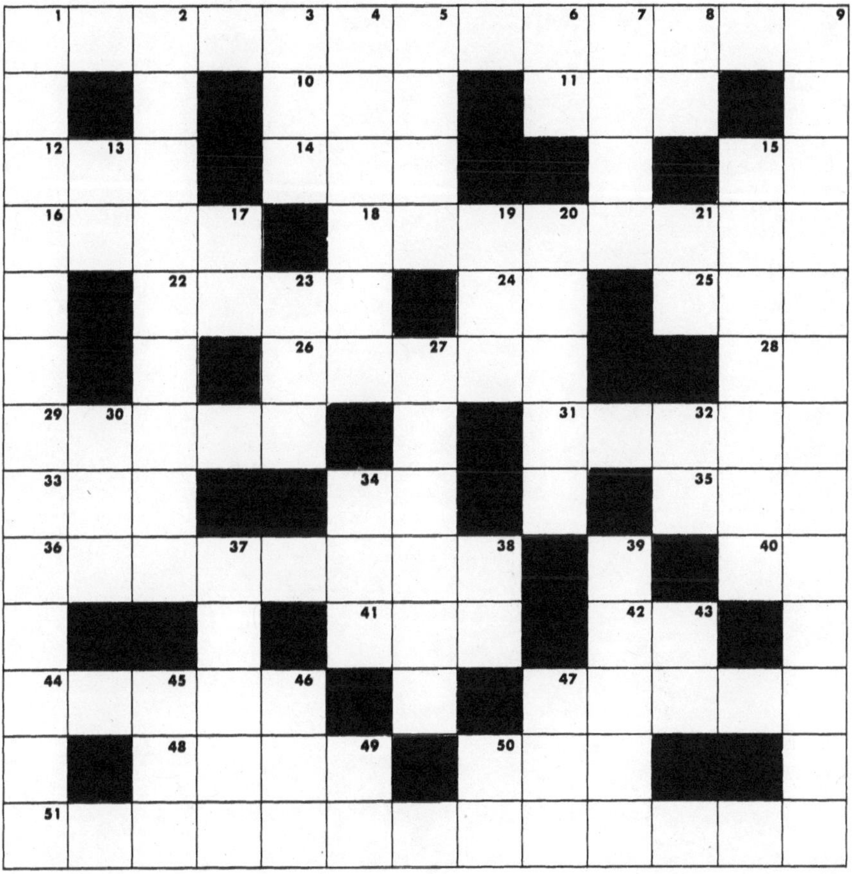

43. -- Ra Ra Boom Dee Ay
45. Police means of finding actors run amok (Abbrev.)
46. Many of these units are needed to light a show
47. First name of *Jumpers* author
49. Et --, Brute!
50. *Variety*'s primary concern (Abbrev.)

The solution will appear in the next issue of *Theatre History Studies.*

Mid-America Theatre Conference Theatre History Symposium 1982

The 1982 Symposium on "Makers of the Modern Theatre" attracted an average of forty persons to each of the seven sessions. While over seventy persons crowded in to hear Professor Robert Findlay and actor Zbigniew Cynkutis on the history and philosophy of Polish Laboratory Theatre, all sessions were very well attended. The Symposium's pronounced international flavor made it extraordinarily appealing. The chair and the panel coordinators wish to thank the MATC Convention Committee for their gracious efforts in making a place for the Symposium on the convention program, and to acknowledge the generous financial assistance of the Excellence Fund of the Graduate School of the University of Missouri-Columbia.

The following are the papers presented at the Theatre History Symposium during the Mid-America Theatre Conference held in Kansas City, Missouri, March 19-21, 1982.

Bank, Rosemarie K.: Lafayette, Indiana
"The Naturalistic Bias in Criticism at the Turn of the Century vs. Lillian Mortimer."

Bristow, Eugene K.: Indiana University
"Let's Hear it from the Losers; or, Chekhov, Komissarzhevskaya, and *The Sea Gull* at St. Petersburg in 1896."

Black, Lendley: University of Kansas
"Michael Chekhov."

Golub, Spencer: University of Virginia
"The Mysteries of the Self: The Visionary Theatre of Nikolai Evreinov."

Finlay, Robert with Zbigniew Cynkutis: University of Kansas-Lawrence
"Growtowski Our Contemporary: Patterns of Mystification/DeMystification."

Hanson, Katherine: Seattle, Washington
"Ibsen's Women Characters and their Feminist Contemporaries."

Harris, Laurilyn J.: Washington State University
"Charles Gilpin: Opening the Way for the American Black Actor."

Harvey, Anne-Charlotte: San Diego State University
"Strindberg's Symbolic Room."

Londré, Felicia H.: University of Missouri-Kansas City
"The Collection Creations of Ariane Mnouchkine."

McDermott, Dana S.: University of California-Riverside
"Robert Edmond Jones and Eugene O'Neill: Two American Visionaries."

McGraw, Rex: University of Nebraska-Lincoln
"The Work of the Actor on a Role: Stanislavski's System of Play Analysis."

Shapiro, Bruce G.: University of South Dakota

"Divine Madness and the Absurd Paradox: Soren Kierkegaard and the Last Five Minutes of Henrik Ibsen's *Peer Gynt*."

Southard, Andrea: University of Maine-Farmington

"Nikolai Okhlopkov: A Magnifying Glass of Soviet Theatre."

Szafkó, Péter: Lajos Kossuth University, Debrecen, Hungary (Indiana University)

"Sándor Hevesi and the Thália Society in Hungary."

Watermeier, Daniel J.: SUNY-Plattsburgh

"Edwin Booth's Performances: New Documentation."

Wegner, Pamela: Wartburg College, Iowa

"Rachel Crothers and the 'New Woman'."

Zatlin-Boring, Phyllis: Rutgers University

"Ana Diosdado and the Contemporary Spanish Theatre."

Zivanovic, Judith: South Dakota State University-Brookings

"Something Borrowed, Something New: The *Verfremdungseffekt* of Bertolt Brecht in Acting."

Theatre History Symposium 1983

The 1983 Theatre History Symposium will be held March 18-20 at the fourth annual Mid-American Theatre Conference in Iowa City, IA. The theme will be *Crosscurrents: The Arts of the Theatre*. Topics will include historical perspectives on the theatre and its relationships to music, painting, film, dance, sculpture, architecture, poetry, and narrative fiction. Send proposals for papers or abstracts to Felicia Londré, Department of Theatre, University of Missouri-Kansas City, 4949 Cherry, Kansas City, Missouri, 64110-2499.